HARRY POTTER AND
THE PRISONER OF AZKABAN

21ST CENTURY FILM ESSENTIALS

Cinema has a storied history, but its story is far from over. 21st Century Film Essentials offers a lively chronicle of cinema's second century, examining the landmark films of our ever-changing moment. Each book makes a case for the importance of a particular contemporary film for artistic, historical, or commercial reasons. The twenty-first century has already been a time of tremendous change in filmmaking the world over, from the rise of digital production and the ascent of the multinational blockbuster to increased vitality in independent filmmaking and the emergence of new voices and talents both on screen and off. The films examined here are the ones that embody and exemplify these changes, crystallizing emerging trends or pointing in new directions. At the same time, they are films that are informed by and help refigure the cinematic legacy of the previous century, showing how film's past is constantly reimagined and rewritten by its present. These are films both familiar and obscure, foreign and domestic; they are new but of lasting value. This series is a study of film history in the making. It is meant to provide a different kind of approach to cinema's story—one written in the present tense.

Donna Kornhaber, *Series Editor*

ALSO IN THE SERIES

Dana Polan, *The LEGO Movie*

Harry Potter and the Prisoner of Azkaban

Patrick Keating

UNIVERSITY OF TEXAS PRESS ✦ AUSTIN

Requests for permission to reproduce material from
this work should be sent to:
    Permissions
    University of Texas Press
    P.O. Box 7819
    Austin, TX 78713-7819
    utpress.utexas.edu/rp-form

∞ The paper used in this book meets the minimum requirements
of ANSI/NISO Z39.48-1992 (R1997) (Permanence of Paper).

Library of Congress Cataloging-in-Publication Data

Names: Keating, Patrick, 1970– author. | Cuarón, Alfonso, film director.
Title: Harry Potter and the prisoner of Azkaban / Patrick Keating.
Description: First edition. | Austin : University of Texas Press, 2021. |
    Series: 21st century film essentials | Includes index.
Identifiers: LCCN 2020044289
    ISBN 978-1-4773-2312-0 (paperback)
    ISBN 978-1-4773-2313-7 (library ebook)
    ISBN 978-1-4773-2314-4 (non-library ebook)
Subjects: LCSH: Cuarón, Alfonso. | Harry Potter and the prisoner of
    Azkaban (Motion picture) | Fantasy films—Production and direction—
    Case studies. | Film adaptations—Production and direction—Case studies.
Classification: LCC PN1997.2.H39 K43 2021 | DDC 823/.92—dc23
LC record available at https://lccn.loc.gov/2020044289

doi:10.7560/323120

Contents

HARRY POTTER AND
THE PRISONER OF AZKABAN

Introduction

When producers approached Alfonso Cuarón to ask if he would consider directing the third *Harry Potter* movie, he was unfamiliar with the series. His friend Guillermo del Toro said, "Don't be stupid. Read them immediately."[1] When Cuarón did so, he was delighted to learn that he loved the books and that *Harry Potter and the Prisoner of Azkaban* was his favorite of the series so far. Taking over directing duties from Chris Columbus, Cuarón committed to the project, which premiered in summer of 2004. The resulting film is more than just a skillful entertainment; it is an essential work of twenty-first-century cinema.

Cuarón's movie (hereafter, *Prisoner of Azkaban*) is an elegant exemplar of several contemporary cinematic trends, including serial storytelling, the rise of the fantasy genre, digital filmmaking, collaborative authorship, and transnational production. Telling one coherent story over the course of eight films, the *Harry Potter* series contributed to an industrywide shift toward complex stories that unfold in ever-expanding fictional worlds—a shift that would reach its culmination on the big screen in the Marvel Cinematic Universe and on the small screen in the complex storytelling that has flourished in recent years on television and streaming services.[2] Alongside the *Lord of the Rings* trilogy, the series changed the balance of genres in Hollywood; as Kristin Thompson explains, the two series "helped raise fantasy from its status as box-office poison to a position at the core of current Hollywood filmmaking."[3] As a work of digital cinema, *Prisoner of Azkaban* provides a model for ambitious filmmakers seeking to insert spectacular fantasy effects and virtual camerawork into their films without compromising the integrity of the story. Cuarón's film demonstrates that it is possible to incorporate an auteur's vision into the collaborative context that such big-budget, serialized filmmaking requires. *Prisoner of Azkaban* is at once a distinctively Cuarón film and a sequel belonging wholly to the *Harry Potter* series.

Outside of Steven Spielberg, it is hard to think of a director who has received so much critical acclaim and who has made a movie that proved to be so popular (grossing nearly $800 million worldwide).[4] Producer David Heyman's decision to hire Cuarón was truly inspired—few expected the British producer to hire a Mexican director whose most recent credit, *Y Tu Mamá También* (2001), had been a Spanish-language film aimed at adult audiences. Cuarón's artistry is visible throughout the film—in his flamboyant long takes, artful motifs, and delicate handling of the cast. But so is the artistry of hundreds of other contributors, from production designer Stuart Craig and costume designer Jany Temime to screenwriter Steve Kloves and composer John Williams. *Prisoner of Azkaban* deserves to be viewed and re-viewed not just because of its bold director but also because it is such a remarkable achievement in collaborative authorship, drawing together a range of crafts to extend and enrich J. K. Rowling's preexisting story-world.[5] The film succeeds marvelously in capturing the most engaging elements of Rowling's novel and translating those traits into cinematic terms. Like its namesake book,

Prisoner of Azkaban has lightness, craft, wonder, and wit. The film is not a scene-for-scene transcription of the novel, but it does justice to its tone.

A key to the film's success lies in a choice that Cuarón and his collaborators made in preproduction: the decision to honor Rowling's approach to point of view. Together, the filmmakers asked: How might a *Harry Potter* film adapt the novel's literary point of view into cinematic terms?

CINEMATIC POINT OF VIEW

As a narrational strategy, the book *Prisoner of Azkaban* follows Harry's adventures in every chapter, and it reveals information about other characters only when Harry encounters those characters himself. As shorthand, one might say that the books are told from Harry's point of view. Although the character of Harry Potter does not narrate the books, he serves as the primary focalizer or filter—that is, as the character whose perceptions mediate the reader's access to the story-world.[6] This technique motivates the text's concealment of key information: Remus Lupin's secret identity as a werewolf; Sirius Black's hidden motivation to find and kill Peter Pettigrew; Hermione Granger's concealed powers as a time traveler. In functional terms these gaps enable the book to produce three quintessential narrative effects: suspense, curiosity, and surprise.[7] Much of Rowling's genius as a writer lies in her ability to devise tension-filled situations and shocking twists.

Embracing Rowling's considerable powers as a storyteller, the filmmakers behind *Prisoner of Azkaban* opted to follow her model by aligning the cinematic point of view closely—but not perfectly—with Harry's own. Cuarón insisted on this approach, and producer Heyman heartily approved. The director explained:

> I felt very strongly that the third film should be told solely from Harry's point of view. I didn't want to see anything Harry wouldn't see or perceive. By point of view, I don't mean that the camera only looks through one character's eyes, but that the core of the story revolves around his growing awareness and his emotions.[8]

Harry does not tell his own story, nor is there any voice-over to reveal his internal thoughts. Even the use of true POV shots is relatively sparing. Still, the film consistently reveals story information only as Harry discovers it. When the film breaks that internal norm, it does so strategically, juxtaposing Harry's perspective with that of other characters, notably his quick-witted classmate Hermione. This governing strategy of telling the story through the mediation of its protagonist sounds obvious, but it is not. Other fantasy film franchises—such as the *Star Wars* movies, the *Lord of the Rings* movies, and the *Avengers* movies—favor an unrestricted approach, cutting freely among multiple protagonists and villains. The remaining seven films in the *Harry Potter* franchise are loosely filtered through Harry's perspective, but they allow a greater variety of deviations in portraying scenes that Harry is not present to see. This does not mean that all of the above-named works are bad films, but it does mean that *Prisoner of Azkaban* is trying something different—and rather difficult. The fact is that movies and novels do not render points of view in the same way. A novel may limit itself to describing only those details that the protagonist notices, but a movie's imagery is typically so dense with detail that it inevitably depicts nuances that the protagonist could not possibly see. So in choosing to limit point of view, Cuarón had set his collaborators a problem. Rather than attempting to show the entire world through Harry's eyes, Cuarón and his collaborators would use the tools of cinema—among them framing, production design, and sound—to emphasize how Harry's perspective on the wizarding world is just that: a perspective, a way of seeing the world that produces gaps as well as genuine insights.

POINT OF VIEW, PERSPECTIVE, AND OTHER KEY TERMS

The film scholar V. F. Perkins has written eloquently about the relationship between worlds and perspectives in the cinema. A film's world "is constituted as a world partly because, within it, there are facts known to all, to many, to few and to none. . . . To be in a world is to know the partiality of knowledge and the boundedness of vision."[9] All films represent their worlds partially, but some films make those limitations a theme of the work. *Prisoner of Azkaban* is such a film. It creates a world, and it shows how that world can never be known fully. To be sure, a commercial imperative lies behind the filmmakers' determination to create a world that expands beyond the borders of its frame. Displaying a world that is richly detailed yet incomplete creates the desire to read more *Harry Potter* books, see more *Harry Potter* films, and visit more *Harry Potter* theme parks. But worldmaking is a basic task of all cinematic storytelling, and *Prisoner of Azkaban* adeptly suggests that its world extends outward in space and backward and forward in time, always leaving more details to be revealed and more secrets to be discovered. Even better, the movie shows how this world, with its own physical laws, social norms, and institutions, may be experienced from different perspectives. Like the book, the movie adopts the principle that Harry's is the primary filtering perspective, but it also takes advantage of the differences between literature and cinema to loosen that principle at a few strategic moments, sometimes by allowing the camera to fly freely through the yards of Hogwarts, sometimes by juxtaposing Harry's experience of events with Hermione's. The end result is not identical to Rowling's text, but it accomplishes an analogous effect, telling the story through Harry while maintaining a hint of ironic distance, thereby mixing sympathy with gentle critique.

Even if the film were a series of subjective shots, it still would articulate a cinematic point of view that differs subtly from Harry's own. As film scholar Deborah Thomas explains, "A film's point of view is clearly not reducible to that of the characters—or even a privileged character—within it, but includes an attitude or orientation toward the various characters (whether one of ironic detachment, sympathetic involvement, moral condemnation, or whatever)."[10] A film develops its orientation in many ways: through camera placement, production design, music, performance, dialogue, and all the other tools at the filmmakers' disposal. These techniques express an attitude toward the film's world. To avoid confusion, my analysis will draw distinctions among several closely related terms. Terms like *position*, *angle*, and *frame* characterize the camera's spatial location, including its virtual position when the shot in question is a digital effect. The term *POV shot* refers to a shot that represents what a character sees, as if the camera were looking through the character's eyes. The term *cinematic point of view* designates the more general cluster of attitudes and orientations that the film develops over time—orientations that are not reducible to the camera's variable positions. (I have drawn the term from the philosopher George M. Wilson.)[11] The term *perspective* relays a character's experience of the story-world, and the terms *focalization* and *filter* refer to the general strategy of motivating gaps in knowledge as gaps in Harry's perspectival understanding of events. On the more fine-grained level, many of the film's specific techniques (camera placement, sound, editing) appeal to *perspectival motivation*, encouraging viewers to understand features of the film as if they were mediated by one or more characters' perspectives.[12]

PRISONER OF AZKABAN AND NARRATIVE THEORY

One of the justifications for conducting a close analysis of *Prisoner of Azkaban* is to better understand the craft and skill that produced it—how a group of master storytellers (Rowling, Cuarón, and the rest) assembled such a marvelous little machine that generates so much tension and such great twists. A related reason is that the film provides a good opportunity to think about more general problems in narrative theory: how focalization might differ in film and literature, how surprise can be combined with suspense, how films allude to spaces and times that they do not show. The movie offers the perfect case study to work through these problems in narrative theory because it is *about* narrative. More specifically, *Prisoner of Azkaban* highlights the tension between two different ways to think about time: as closed and as open. In the context of literature, the theorist Gary Saul Morson has explained the distinction and its importance. Within a closed conception of time, every event is determined; things could not have happened any other way. Within an open conception of time, chance and contingency remain present; each event becomes meaningful because it could have happened otherwise.[13] Although Morson uses the distinction to deepen his analysis of Tolstoy, *Prisoner of Azkaban* manages to address these same philosophical ideas through the vehicle of an elegantly accessible children's film. Near the beginning of the film, the professor of divination, Sybil Trelawney, champions the idea of closed time by claiming the ability to predict the future, as if nothing can be done to change the course of events. Hermione scoffs at the very idea of prophecy, but Harry is strangely drawn to the idea, which seems so relevant to his status as the Chosen One. Near the end of the film, Harry and Hermione get the chance to prove that events may happen differently—not just by taking decisive actions in the future but by intervening in the past with the aid of time travel.

The film's ultimate achievements rest on its ability to tie together these three salient traits: its skillful use of Harry as a mediating perspective; its energetic mixture of suspense, surprise, and curiosity; and its careful weighing of two competing conceptions of time. These three traits work together. First, by filtering much of the story through Harry, the film creates gaps in knowledge—gaps that are crucial to the production of suspense, surprise, and curiosity. Second, by generating these powerful feelings, the film turns the abstract opposition between open time and closed time into something viewers can experience; the intense feeling of suspense is an indication that open time is in effect, since open time requires the future to remain in doubt. Third, by opposing closed time with open time, the film imposes a thematic structure on its handling of perspective, underscoring the gradual shift from the exclusive focus on Harry, who is tempted by the fatalism of closed time, to a more inclusive focus that juxtaposes Harry's perspective with Hermione's, with Hermione cast as a champion of open time. The three accomplishments form one unified achievement.

IN PRAISE OF COLLABORATIVE AUTHORSHIP

Who deserves credit for this achievement? Rowling? Cuarón? How about the screenwriter, the cinematographer, the set decorator, and the costume designer? This book argues: all of the above. As a big-budget franchise film, *Prisoner of Azkaban* relies on a collaborative model of authorship, whereby single-film contributors like Cuarón must work with multifilm contributors like production designer Stuart Craig. To be sure, Cuarón is to be credited for eliciting the very best work from his team, and he had a special hand in designing the film's exceptionally intricate *découpage*. But this book situates Cuarón's contributions as an auteur within the context of a larger group. An initial section on J. K. Rowling's handling of literary point of view leads to an analysis of Steve Kloves's screenplay, which reshapes the book according to the logic of Hollywood plot structure. The next section is more traditionally auteurist in its focus on Cuarón's camerawork, but this is followed by a section treating the film's remarkable actors (young and old) as coauthors of the series. The subsequent section on production design, costumes, and lighting explains how the richly detailed environment becomes world-like by evoking spaces and times that are left unexplored. A concluding section on sound design and music compares the worldbuilding power of the film's richly textured ambiences and effects to the rhetorical power of the film's highly motivic score.

This craft-by-craft progression implicitly endorses the idea of collaborative authorship. More abstractly, it locates the unfolding analysis within a framework drawn from narrative theory, for the progression of this book also follows a rough trajectory, moving (with some zigzagging and backtracking) from perspective to world to rhetorical address. A narrative film aims to produce effects of suspense, surprise, and curiosity, but it does so through the mediating layer of its world—a world always represented through a particular cinematic point of view.

Point of View in the Novels

Perhaps the most immediate trait of the *Harry Potter* movies is their narrative drive; they tell such lively stories. The movies are funny, fast-moving, and a little dark, like the books on which they are based. My analysis begins with Rowling's novels, for the simple reason that Rowling is one of the primary authors of the film. She did not design the sets or organize the camerawork, and she did not even receive a screenplay credit.[1] But her imprint is all over the movies, which deliver the same tone and twists as the books on which they are based. This section considers all seven of Rowling's books before turning to the challenge of adapting *Prisoner of Azkaban* specifically.

For readers unfamiliar with the books, a short summary is in order. The series tells the tale of Harry Potter, an orphan whose parents were killed by the evil wizard Voldemort when Harry was an infant. Each book follows a familiar structure. Typically, the first section depicts Harry's miserable existence with the awful Muggle family the Dursleys. ("Muggle" is the term for nonmagical people.) Next, the school year begins, and Harry goes off to Hogwarts, a special school for wizards. There Harry deals with several recurring plots: his confrontations with the bullying student Draco Malfoy, his hatred for the mysterious teacher Severus Snape, his admiration for the benevolent headmaster Albus Dumbledore, and his ongoing friendship with his fellow students Hermione Granger and Ron Weasley. Most dramatically, Harry faces some threat on his life, either from Voldemort directly or from one of the Dark Lord's agents. At the end of each novel, Harry defeats the threat with the direct and indirect help of his friends and teachers, and the school year ends.

This summary of the novels' recurring features may make the books sound overly formulaic, but in fact Rowling varies the formula each time. Each year Harry meets at least one new professor (typically the Defense Against the Dark Arts professor), who may be benevolent, malevolent, or some complicated combination of the two. Each year Harry learns at least one new magical skill, which he puts to use in the climactic confrontation scene. Each year Harry grows a bit older, and so he experiences ever-increasing levels of teenage angst and romantic confusion. More generally, the books grow longer and more serious over the years, especially after *Goblet of Fire*, the central book in the seven-book series.

The third book, *Prisoner of Azkaban*, is the only one in which Voldemort does not appear. Instead, Harry faces two closely related threats. First, he learns that Sirius Black has escaped from Azkaban to kill him. This news sparks a desire for revenge when Harry learns that Black is the one who betrayed his parents to Voldemort those many years ago. Second, Harry encounters the dementors, prison guards who will harm Harry if he gets in the way of their pursuit of Black. When Harry gets his chance to kill Black, he learns that Black had been falsely accused all along. The real culprit was Peter Pettigrew, who has spent the last several years pretending to be Ron's pet rat Scabbers. As Harry deals with these twin threats, several other subplots unfold: Harry befriends the new Defense Against the Dark Arts teacher, Lupin, who turns out to be a werewolf; Draco uses his connections to get the hippogriff Buckbeak sentenced to death after the creature deals him a minor injury in Professor Rubeus Hagrid's Care of Magical Creatures class; and Professor Minerva McGonagall gives Hermione a time-travel device so she can attend even more classes. In the end these storylines converge marvelously when Hermione and Harry use the time-travel device to rescue Buckbeak and save Sirius, with the help of the Patronus charm that Harry learns from Lupin.

In a notorious opinion piece titled "Can 35 Million Book Buyers Be Wrong? Yes," the great literary critic Harold Bloom denounced J. K. Rowling's work. He charged that the first book (the only one he had read) was not well written and that it lacked an "authentic imaginative vision"; its only achievement was to merge the preexisting worlds of fantasy and mythology with the preexisting form of the English schoolboy novel.[2] I agree that Rowling's prose can be predictable, and I certainly do not want to endorse everything Rowling has written, particularly on Twitter. But I think that Bloom seriously underrates Rowling's literary achievement. Her books feature vivid characters, crafty plot twists, and a brilliant sense of humor, and they allude to an extraordinarily wide range of literary sources, including Greek mythology, Shakespeare, and Jane Austen.[3] Crucial to my argument, Rowling displays an expert command of an important authorial skill: managing point of view. After relying on an omniscient narrator for certain parts of the first book, Rowling committed to a strategy in the second book that she would follow for the next several volumes: filtering the story through Harry's point of view without telling it in his voice. In other words, Rowling set herself a rule. She would imagine a wizarding world of extraordinary complexity, but she would introduce each corner of that world when and only when Harry experienced it. There are no scenes with giant spiders until Harry encounters them; there are no scenes with horn-tailed dragons until Harry learns he has to face one. *Chamber of Secrets*, *Prisoner of Azkaban*, *Goblet of Fire*, and *Order of the Phoenix* all adhere strictly to this rule; the other volumes contain some strategic exceptions, but they too control point of view very tightly, selectively shifting the point of view to another character for just one chapter at a time.

Considering Rowling's writerly achievement first will set the stage for my analysis of the film as a triumphant work of cinematic adaptation. Cuarón's idea seemed simple enough—just put Harry in every scene—but in fact the director required his collaborators to wrestle with some of the foundational problems of narrative filmmaking: How does a film transfer the novelistic technique to the cinema? What does the film gain when it does so? What does it lose?

HARRY AS A FILTER

Narrative theorists have proposed many different names for the writing strategy that Rowling has adopted. Perhaps the most common term is *focalization*, which Gérard Genette introduced to draw a distinction between "who speaks" and "who sees."[4] Without writing the story in the first person (which is a matter of voice), an author might focalize the events through the perspective of a specific character. Henry James's *The Ambassadors* offers a classic illustration. Strether does not narrate the story, but the book describes only those events that

Strether is present to witness. Far from allowing the reader to identify with Strether unproblematically, the tactic exposes—at first gradually and then suddenly—the extent to which the American Strether misunderstands the European world he encounters. Seeking to draw an even sharper distinction between narrators and focalizing characters, the narrative theorist Seymour Chatman has proposed the terms *slant* and *filter*. The former refers to the attitudes of the narrator who tells the story; the latter refers to the perceptions of a character who experiences the story's world from within. As Chatman explains, filter "seems a good term for capturing something of the mediating function of a character's consciousness—perception, cognition, emotion, reverie—as events are experienced from a space within the story world"[5] A book might shift rapidly from one filter to another, or it might use one character as the primary filter from beginning to end. When the character's perceptions turn out to be systematically wrong, the character becomes a *fallible filter*; such a character's misguided assumptions may emerge as a primary subject of the story.[6] Chatman offers Jane Austen's *Emma* as a paradigmatic example. With a few exceptions, the bulk of the book is filtered through Emma, who systematically misreads other characters' intentions and situations. Understanding the book involves understanding that the narrator's slant/attitude toward the filter/protagonist is highly critical.

J. K. Rowling has cited Jane Austen as her favorite author and *Emma* as her favorite book, which she once described as "the most skillfully managed mystery I've ever read."[7] Rowling's *Harry Potter* books are also mysteries of a sort, and they adopt Austen's narrative technique. In *Prisoner of Azkaban* the mystery surrounding the gift of a broom seems to be directly modeled on an episode in *Emma* surrounding the gift of a piano. Although Harry is a more trustworthy filter than Emma or Strether, his fallibility structures the text in significant ways. Raised by relatives in the Muggle world, Harry begins the series unfamiliar with the norms and mores of the wizarding world. Sharing Harry's ignorance, the reader must learn about the inhabitants, history, and rituals of that world as Harry learns about them. During his ensuing encounters with the wizarding world, Harry's judgments change considerably, in the manner of someone experiencing culture shock. He initially overestimates the goodness of the wizarding world, which seems preferable to the Muggle world in every way. Gradually, he comes to realize that the wizarding world is as problematic as the Muggle world is—not just because the magical world contains evil wizards like Voldemort who want to kill him, but because its institutions seem thoroughly corrupt. The political system rewards smooth-talking opportunists like Cornelius Fudge, and the newspaper industry favors the tabloid headlines crafted by celebrity liars like Rita Skeeter; even worse, the justice system convicts innocent people like Sirius Black and subjects them to the terrors of the dementors, and the economic system relies on the enslavement of house-elves. As a filter with a generally reliable moral compass, Harry sooner or later recognizes the corruption of these institutions, thereby guiding readers to condemn the institutions as well.

Harry's fallibility enables the construction of the novels' various mystery plots. He routinely overlooks or misinterprets clues that turn out to be lurking plot twists. The choice of Harry as a filter may seem obvious in retrospect, but Rowling could have structured her novels in many different ways. She could have chosen Ron as a Dr. Watson–like filter, observing

Harry through the eyes of a character who is considerably less knowledgeable than the protagonist; or she could have chosen the more Sherlockian Hermione as a filter, observing Harry through the eyes of a character who solves several mysteries sooner than he does; or she could have chosen an unfiltered, omniscient point of view that skips from Harry to Voldemort to McGonagall to Snape to Lupin to everyone in between. Indeed, the first book, *Harry Potter and the Sorcerer's Stone* (known as *Harry Potter and the Philosopher's Stone* outside the US, where the title was changed for commercial reasons), opens with such an omniscient technique, as in this passage: "When Mr. and Mrs. Dursley woke up on the dull, grey Tuesday our story starts, there was nothing about the cloudy sky outside to suggest that strange and mysterious things would soon be happening all over the country."[8] Not only does the narration describe the Dursleys before Harry is around to witness them; it gives the reader advance warning of future events that the Dursleys cannot possibly predict.

By the start of the second book, Rowling has committed rigorously to the filtering principle. Harry does not narrate his own story, but the narration remains tightly restricted to Harry's range of awareness. Just before the climactic battle with the basilisk, a miscast spell causes some stones to crumble in a tunnel, forming a wall between Harry, on one side, and Ron and the preening professor Gilderoy Lockhart on the other.

> "I'm here!" came Ron's muffled voice from behind the rockfall. "I'm okay—this git's not, though—he got blasted by the wand—"
>
> There was a dull thud and a loud "ow!" It sounded as though Ron had just kicked Lockhart in the shins.[9]

Rather than tell us that Ron kicked Lockhart in the shins, Rowling's prose describes only what Harry hears, and then it explains what Harry infers on the basis of that perception. The point of view remains on Harry's side of the wall. An even more dramatic example occurs in the fourth book, *Goblet of Fire*. During the Triwizard Tournament, all four competitors must steal an egg from a dragon. Harry remains inside a tent while the other competitors face the challenge one by one. Rather than follow the competitors outside, the narration remains with Harry, who must guess what each competitor is doing based on the cheers from the crowd.[10] Forgoing the opportunity to narrate four thrilling dragon battles in succession, the novel aims for the subtler pleasures of characterization by describing a boy sitting nervously in a tent.

THREE LIMITATIONS

Committing to this strategy requires certain sacrifices on Rowling's part, placing limitations on the reader's access to three distinct types of information: what other characters are thinking, what happened in the past, and what will happen in the future. First, the filtering technique severely limits the reader's access to other characters' minds. When Rowling wants to describe another character's thoughts or emotions, her prose describes only those traits that remain visible or audible to Harry, as in *Prisoner of Azkaban*, which describes Hermione's response to a mean-spirited critique from Professor Snape: "Hermione went very red, put down her hand, and stared at the floor with her eyes full of tears."[11] Here, Hermione's emotions are visible in her behavior. When characters conceal their internal states from Harry, Rowling's prose remains unforthcoming, leaving the reader (and Harry) to guess what the character is thinking. The limiting pattern is so consistent that Rowling can joke about it, as in this scene from *Order of the Phoenix*:

> Hermione pulled the newspaper back toward her, closed it, glared for a moment at the pictures of the ten escaped Death Eaters on the front, then leapt to her feet.
>
> "Where are you going?" said Ron, startled.
>
> "To send a letter," said Hermione, swinging her bag onto her shoulder. "It . . . well, I don't know whether . . . but it's worth trying . . . and I'm the only one who can."
>
> "I hate it when she does that," grumbled Ron as he and Harry got up from the table and made their own, slower way out of the Great Hall. "Would it kill her to tell us what she's up to? It'd take her about ten more seconds."[12]

By revealing that Hermione has had an idea without disclosing what it is, Rowling turns an apparent limitation into an advantage, generating curiosity about Hermione's plan and suspense about whether or not it will succeed, along with a good dose of humor for readers who recognize that Rowling pulls this trick in almost every book.

Note that Rowling's commitment to using Harry as a filter still gives her considerable freedom when it comes to reporting Harry's own thoughts. Sometimes the narration reports Harry's thoughts indirectly, as in this passage from *Prisoner of Azkaban*: "A hatred such as he had never known before was coursing through Harry like poison."[13] Sometimes the narration quotes thoughts directly, as in *Order of the Phoenix*, where Harry experiences an ugly mixture of doubt and jealousy: *"Well, Ron and Hermione were with me most of the time,* said the voice in Harry's head. *Not all the time, though,* Harry argued with himself. *They didn't fight Quirrell with me.*[14] And occasionally the narration refuses to grant access to Harry's thoughts at all, as in *Half-Blood Prince*, where the narration discloses that Harry has a plan to bolster Ron's self-confidence as Gryffindor's goalkeeper without revealing what that plan is.[15] To borrow two terms from David Bordwell, the range remains restricted to Harry, but the depth is variable, frequently dipping into Harry's mind but occasionally withholding access.[16] Rowling juggles these options to produce a wide range of effects, from the management of her celebrated plot twists to the development of her increasingly serious themes. In one of the bleakest books in the series, *Order of the Phoenix*, Harry sees a sculpture when he enters the Ministry of Magic. Rowling's prose ("Tallest of them all was a noble-looking wizard") evokes the sense of wonder that Harry feels as he enters the revered institution.[17] But Harry soon gets a lesson in how corrupt that institution really is, and the second description of Harry's encounter with the statue ("He looked up into the handsome wizard's face, but up close, Harry thought he looked rather weak and foolish") vividly conveys his disillusionment.[18]

A second limitation inherent to the filtering technique is a restriction on exposition. A novel with an omniscient narrator may freely skip back in time to inform the reader about previous events that are relevant to the ongoing story, but a novel that sticks closely to one character's perspective must make do with what the character remembers in the moment. This limitation poses a particular problem when the books form a series. *Sorcerer's Stone* gets around the problem with passages of omniscient narration, but in later books Rowling finds ways to remind her readers what happened in the earlier volumes via Harry's mediation. In some passages she solves the problem via dialogue, as when Harry explains the rules of Quidditch to an inquisitive Colin Creevey in *Chamber of Secrets*.[19] In other passages Rowling uses Harry's mental states to provide needed exposition. In *Goblet of Fire* Mad-Eye Moody explains the killing curse to the class, which prompts Harry to retreat into his own dark thoughts: "Harry had been picturing his parents' deaths over and over again for three years now, ever since he found out they had been murdered, ever since he'd found out what had happened that night: Wormtail had betrayed his parents' whereabouts to Voldemort."[20] Rather than rely on an omniscient narrator to explain this crucial backstory without a mediating agent, Rowling filters our access to the scene through Harry, who is recalling crucial facts about his own history. Again, Rowling turns a potential limitation into a storytelling advantage, preparing for the fourth volume's climactic scene with Wormtail and Voldemort while underscoring the revenge theme that runs throughout the series.

If this second limitation concerns the past, a third limitation concerns the future. In a previously quoted passage from the opening to *Sorcerer's Stone*, the omniscient narrator prepares us to expect "strange and mysterious things" to happen all over the country. Notice how the narrator has jumped ahead to future events, offering the sort of insight about coming events that the main character (Harry, still an infant) could not possibly possess. Narrative theorists call such passages, where the narrator breaks the chronology and leaps to the future, *prolepses*. As Genette explains, pure prolepses are somewhat rare in traditional novels because they undercut suspense by revealing the ending in advance.[21] They are particularly rare in highly focalized novels, since the filter typically cannot see the future, even if the narrator can. To get around this problem, a novelist might employ tentative or partial prolepses, generating suspense by hinting at various possible outcomes. Because the *Harry Potter* books are largely restricted to Harry's perspective, these hints must be delivered via an account of his future-oriented experiences, as in *Goblet of Fire*, where Harry rolls over in bed and imagines winning the Triwizard Tournament, thereby allowing the reader to imagine a future event that does indeed come to pass, though without the happy emotional consequences that Harry expects.[22]

Thus far I have emphasized how the books' narration relies on Harry's words and thoughts to get around three limitations posed by the filtering technique: access to others' thoughts, the exposition of past events, and prolepses about the future. But Rowling has an even more powerful way of getting around these limitations: magic. Harry Potter is not just any filtering protagonist, but a protagonist with magical powers. These powers extend Rowling's storytelling abilities considerably. Indeed, one way to imagine the wizarding world is to think of it as a collection of narratological devices, allowing Rowling to explore ever vaster expanses of this world while adhering to her self-imposed obligation to tell the story from Harry's perspective.[23] A partial list of those devices would include:

1. The Pensieve, a bowl of liquid that allows Harry to experience the memories of Albus Dumbledore, Professor Slughorn, and other characters, thereby allowing the narration to sneak past the regulation against entering the minds of other characters and to escape the limitation on delivering exposition for events that happened when Harry was not present.[24]
2. The dream at the beginning of *Goblet of Fire*, representing Voldemort's murder of the gardener, in a

scene that initially seems like a violation of the filtering strategy but turns out to be a continuation of it, on the grounds that Harry and Voldemort share a mental connection.

3. The even more disturbing dream in *Order of the Phoenix*, representing the snake's attempted murder of Mr. Weasley from the snake's perspective; again, the shift to another character's optical experience seems like a complete violation of the Harry-as-filter principle, but it is justified by the fact that Voldemort has learned to manipulate Harry's thoughts.

4. The lessons that Snape teaches Harry about the arts of Legilimens (reading other minds) and Occlumens (blocking others from reading one's own mind), which provide motivation for various scenes in which Harry tries to understand others and/or realizes that someone else knows what he is thinking.

5. The boggart, which takes the shape of its victims' fears, and the Mirror of Erised, which represents a character's desires ("Erised" being "desire" spelled backwards); both devices take an internal state and make it visible.

6. Professor Trelawney's prophecies, which announce several future events while keeping their status ambiguous, since Trelawney's gift for predicting the future remains the subject of considerable debate.

NARRATIVE DYNAMICS

Such magic extends the reach of Harry's range of knowledge, but he remains prone to mistakes, and Rowling exploits his well-intentioned fallibility to deliver her mysteries and twists.

Rowling followed the *Harry Potter* novels with a series of mystery novels released under the pen name Robert Galbraith, but in fact she was something of a mystery novelist all along. In all seven of the *Harry Potter* books, the protagonist must solve a puzzle, as in *Chamber of Secrets*, when Harry must discover what is causing his classmates to turn to stone, or in *Half-Blood Prince*, when Harry must figure out why Draco keeps disappearing from the Marauder's Map. In all seven books Rowling executes bait-and-switch maneuvers worthy of Agatha Christie, as in *Sorcerer's Stone*, which tricks the reader into thinking that Snape is trying to harm Harry only to reveal that Quirrell is the culprit, or in *Goblet of Fire*, which tricks the reader into thinking that Mad-Eye Moody is an erratic but sincere ally only to reveal that he is a Death Eater in disguise. Harry spends the bulk of each novel sifting through partial information and searching for more. He often must rely on Hermione or Dumbledore to fill in the blanks. In many of the novels the central mystery is explicitly framed as a question, as in *Deathly Hallows*, where Harry asks himself, "Was there something he had missed in the long talks with Dumbledore last year? Ought he to know what it all meant?"[25] Rowling's narrative technique aligns the reader with his situation, grasping for clues, guessing at answers, and, more than once, falling prey to deception.

The alignment is never total. Harry remains in his world, and the reader remains outside, encountering the world through the text. Theorists have long insisted that narratives involve two sequences: the sequence of events happening in the story-world and the sequence of the text as it reveals or conceals aspects of that story-world. As Meir Sternberg explains, narrativity "entails an interplay between the one sequence's flow of developments and the other's flow of disclosures—between the two great sources of narrative change, in the world itself and in our knowledge about it, respectively—so as to keep the reader's mind on the move all along."[26] Narratives manipulate this interplay, with its inherent gaps between sequences, to produce three characteristic effects: suspense, curiosity, and surprise. Suspense leads the reader to look forward to a gap in the future, hoping and/or fearing a variety of outcomes. Curiosity causes the reader to look backward to a gap in the past, as in a mystery that passes over key facts about who committed the crime and why. Surprise is similar to curiosity in that it concerns a gap in the past, but it is also different, because the gap does not even seem like a gap until it is revealed. The reader of a mystery may spend hundreds of pages wondering what happened on the day of the crime; the reader of a novel with a surprising plot twist may realize, suddenly, that the previous hundred pages had been misleading all along.[27]

In my view, Rowling's mastery of the dynamics of suspense, curiosity, and surprise is her greatest talent, and that talent is on full display throughout *Prisoner of Azkaban*. If the film adaptation is to succeed at anything, it must get these dynamics right. The primary storyline is a suspense plot. Harry learns that Sirius Black has escaped from Azkaban, and he fears that Sirius will try to kill him. But that suspense plot turns into a surprise plot. Harry thinks that he understands a crucial event in the past—that Sirius murdered a crowd of people, including Peter Pettigrew—but he learns that his understanding is mistaken: Pettigrew committed the murder. By using Harry as a filter, Rowling amplifies the feelings of suspense and surprise. The reader shares Harry's uncertainty about Sirius as a future danger (producing suspense) as well as Harry's misunderstanding of Sirius as a criminal (producing surprise). That said, the reader's fears remain distinct from Harry's. Knowing that *Prisoner of Azkaban* is the third book in a series, the reader can hardly expect Harry to get killed off by Sirius, no matter how worried Harry might be. Rowling addresses this potential flaw by taking the danger plot and turning it into a morality plot. In the early chapters Harry has no intention of confronting Sirius. After he learns of Sirius's alleged crimes, Harry resolves to kill him. This opens up a suspense plot of an entirely different sort. Now the question is not "Will Sirius kill Harry?" but "Will Harry give in to his darker urges and commit an act of violence that he will regret?" Many commentators have observed that the books' themes grow darker as the series progresses, and *Prisoner of Azkaban* is an important step in this progression, raising the possibility that the good-natured Harry will become more like his double, Voldemort.[28]

Rowling's other plots carry their own narrative dynamics. Many of them involve suspense: Will the dementors harm Harry in their efforts to capture Sirius? Will the Ministry execute Buckbeak? Will Trelawney's prediction that a servant of Voldemort will rejoin his master come true?[29] Several plots incite curiosity by introducing a mystery only to deliver a surprising solution. Curiosity: Why does Hermione sometimes pop up in the middle of class? Surprise: She can travel in time! Curiosity: Why does Ron's pet rat Scabbers disappear? Surprise: He is Peter Pettigrew in animal form! Curiosity: Is there something wrong with Professor Lupin? Surprise: He's a werewolf! Curiosity: Why is a black dog following Harry? Surprise: The dog has been Sirius all along! Curiosity: Who rescues Harry with a Patronus charm? Surprise: Harry casts the charm himself! These proliferating storylines might seem like too much for one book or movie, but Rowling's narrative technique ties them all together neatly, as when the seemingly minor question of why Hermione keeps appearing and disappearing in class sets up the crucial twist that allows Hermione and Harry to rescue Sirius.

Several threads come together in the Shrieking Shack scene in chapter 17, a dazzling display of narrative dynamics, swerving back and forth from suspense to surprise to curiosity and back again. The movie turns this chapter into one of its best scenes, featuring Gary Oldman's delightfully overwrought performance as Sirius. First, we learn that Sirius was the black dog (surprise). This revelation suggests that Sirius is preparing to kill Harry (suspense). But then Harry gets the upper hand, and it seems like Harry might kill Sirius (suspense of a deeper sort). Then Lupin arrives and reveals that he is in league with Sirius (surprise, along with a new line of suspense about Lupin as a possible threat). Then Hermione reveals that Lupin is a werewolf (resolving the previously established curiosity about his odd behavior). Lupin explains that he and Sirius are after Peter Pettigrew, still in animal form as Ron's rat (a big surprise, revealing that the previous surprise about Lupin's seeming malevolence was thoroughly misleading). Amazingly, Rowling delivers all of these twists in the span of just ten pages.

Prisoner of Azkaban's plots also fit into the larger architecture of the series. The first book introduces several suspense questions that subsequent books must maintain. Will Voldemort kill Harry? Will the wizarding world prove to be better or worse than the nonmagical world? Will Harry find an appropriate father figure? Will Harry, Hermione, and Ron learn to work together? Initiating the shift to more serious themes that become more pronounced at the end of the next volume, *Prisoner of Azkaban* exposes the wizarding world's institutions as fundamentally unjust. The Lupin plot, which culminates in the beloved teacher getting sacked for being a werewolf, serves as a metaphorical critique of discrimination against people with stigmatizing diseases or disabilities, and the dementor plot, which reveals the brutality of the wizarding prison system, serves as a more literal critique of the politics of incarceration.[30] Meanwhile, Harry continues his ongoing search for father figures: after gaining and losing Lupin as a mentor, Harry emerges from the book with a new godfather in Sirius Black, whose virtues and flaws will become more apparent in the next two volumes. As for the Harry-Hermione-Ron storyline, *Prisoner of Azkaban* gives Hermione a more active role, especially when she uses her Time Turner to bring Harry back in time to rescue Buckbeak and Sirius. This marks a notable departure from the previous book, which had received justified criticism for sidelining Hermione in various ways. (She sat out the Polyjuice adventure after accidentally transforming herself into a cat, and she failed to enter the Chamber of Secrets with Harry and Ron because a basilisk had turned her to stone.)[31]

THE DYNAMICS OF OPEN TIME

Hermione's actions in *Prisoner of Azkaban* develop one of the series' crucial themes: the theme of time. This theme appears explicitly in Professor Trelawney's divination class. By telling her students that she can predict the future, Trelawney proposes a theory of time as closed, as if events are foreordained to happen. For all his agency as the protagonist, Harry seems drawn to this vision of the world; he is seduced into the belief that he has been chosen by fate. Hermione, normally so deferential to her teachers, completely rejects Trelawney's abilities

and her philosophy of closed time. Hermione's actions support
the alternative theory that time is open, especially when she
helps Harry alter the past. Rather than resolve the issue decisively, Rowling maintains a careful balance. Trelawney may
be a fraud, but she delivers one prophecy about the servant of
Voldemort that turns out to be true. Harry and Hermione may
be able to save Black from the dementors, but they learn that
it was Harry who cast the Patronus charm in the first place.
Later books will return to the same theme. The entire plot of
Order of the Phoenix revolves around a prophecy; in the subsequent book Dumbledore remonstrates with Harry for giving
the prophecy too much credence.[32] The headmaster passion-
ately insists that actions count for more than predictions.[33]

In staging this philosophical dispute, Rowling again shows
her debt to her literary precursors, including Jane Austen.
Gary Saul Morson argues that the contrast between closed
time (in which events are predetermined) and open time (in
which choice, chance, and contingency may shape the course
of events) was a major concern of the nineteenth-century
novel:

> Many novels do palpably represent a world in which
> choice matters and creativity is real. Reading George
> Eliot, Jane Austen, and Turgenev, we sense, as we do in
> life, the presentness of the present and the multiplicity
> of possible futures. We experience suspense, a sign of our
> belief in alternate possibilities, and judge actions that, it
> seems evident, might have been different.[34]

Note the importance of the reader's experience to Morson's
account. Apart from writing a few speeches for Dumbledore,
Rowling does not develop the theme by putting long

monologues into the mouths of her characters; she develops the theme by telling a story filled with suspense and surprise. Suspense requires the reader to make predictions about the future (for instance, by guessing one possible positive outcome and one possible negative outcome), but it also requires that those predictions remain uncertain.[35] Surprise tricks the reader into assuming that some facts about the fictional world are established truth—only to expose a hidden gap in knowledge, thereby warning the reader not to take established facts for granted.

The movies add another twist to this account of Rowling's narrative dynamics because they manage to generate suspense even though millions of readers knew the outcome in advance. Such a twist invokes a classic problem in aesthetics, known as the paradox of suspense: If suspense requires uncertainty, why do we feel it so strongly when we know the ending already? To resolve the problem, it is useful to remember that there are two distinct levels of uncertainty at play: there is uncertainty at the level of the fictional world (where Harry might or might not get killed by a troll or a basilisk or a werewolf), and there is uncertainty at the level of reading (where the reader might or might not know the ending already). When we reach the end of a novel or movie, we have achieved a fuller understanding of the fictional world—which includes the understanding that Harry faced real danger. He was not killed by a troll or a basilisk or a werewolf, but he came awfully close. For philosopher Noël Carroll, imagining a chain of events charged with such uncertainty is sufficient to produce suspense, even if we are reading a novel for the second time or watching a movie for the tenth.[36]

Novel to Screenplay

J. K. Rowling would later tell a story about her first meeting with Steve Kloves, who was in line to write the screenplay for *Sorcerer's Stone*. They were sitting in a restaurant with a Hollywood producer who only pretended to have read the book. Then:

> Steve turned to me while food was being ordered and said quietly, "You know who my favorite character is?" I looked at him, red hair included, and I thought, "You're going to say Ron. Please, please don't say Ron—Ron's so easy to love." And he said, "Hermione." At which point, under my standoffish, mistrusting exterior, I just melted, because if he got Hermione, he got the books.[1]

Kloves went on to adapt seven of the eight Potter films. (Michael Goldenberg adapted *Order of the Phoenix.*) Throughout the process Kloves faced the challenge of condensation; for *Prisoner of Azkaban*, he had to turn a 453-page book into a movie that runs 130 minutes before the closing credits roll. In interviews Kloves joked that the screenwriter's burden of economizing made him hated around the world, as fans would blame him every time a movie failed to include a favorite detail from the novels.[2] Rowling told Kloves not to worry. She understood that cuts were necessary; all she asked was that he "stay true to the characters."[3]

Cuarón also pushed Kloves to remove as much exposition as possible and to keep the focus squarely on Harry.[4] Most of the resulting trims to *Prisoner of Azkaban* strike me as perfectly justified. Kloves cut or trimmed a long-simmering mystery about who sent Harry the Firebolt, a surprising number of scenes involving Crookshanks the cat, and the usual series of Quidditch matches that go on forever.[5] In my view, the only significant loss is the backstory to the Marauder's Map: the screenplay contains no explicit mention that Moony, Wormtail, Padfoot, and Prongs are Remus Lupin, Peter Pettigrew, Sirius Black, and James Potter. Kloves skillfully tightened the remaining storylines by cutting assorted repetitions. There are fewer sightings of the black dog and fewer references to Hermione taking so many classes at once. Such judicious trims allowed Kloves to expand key chapters—most notably, the time-travel episode from chapter 21, which becomes a twenty-minute set piece in the finished film.

ACT STRUCTURE

These adjustments tighten the story, but they do not get to the core of Kloves's achievement. As a screenwriter, Kloves had the responsibility to address a particular storytelling problem—the problem of Harry's passivity. Hollywood's screenwriting gurus have insisted for decades that a movie's protagonist must be active, "locking the conflict" by committing to solve the problem at any cost.[6] But the narrative structure of the *Potter* books often assigns greater agency to other characters: the villains who conspire against Harry, the teachers who tell him what he needs to know, and the friends who help him along the way. In Rowling's book Harry is explicitly not searching for Sirius, and he does very little to uncover the true identities of the black dog, Scabbers, and Lupin. The book describes several clues from Harry's perspective, but he quickly misinterprets them and lets the matter drop. When Snape gives Lupin a potion, Harry makes the easy assumption that Snape is trying to take Lupin's job as the instructor for Defense Against the Dark Arts.[7] When Scabbers loses his hair, Harry mistakenly supposes that the rat is just getting old.[8] When Sirius fails to kill Ron during a nighttime attack, Harry wonders why, but he does nothing to resolve the mystery.[9] As usual, Hermione proves to be a better investigator than Harry. It is only in the climactic scene, when Harry successfully casts the Patronus charm to send the dementors away, that he emerges as an active hero.

Kloves might have addressed this problem by intensifying Harry's agency—perhaps by adding scenes of Harry ransacking Hogwarts to locate his enemy Sirius or by inserting a subplot centered on Harry investigating Lupin's strange behavior. Instead, Kloves does something more character-driven, embracing the particular mixture of heroic agency and passive apprenticeship that defines Harry in the books. The screenplay's structure centers on one storyline that requires Harry to be active; layered around this central storyline are several other storylines that foreground Harry's reactive qualities, allowing supporting characters like Hermione and Lupin to come to the fore.

The central storyline involves Harry's conflict with the dementors, and this plot follows a canonical screenplay structure. A brief summary of Hollywood screenwriting norms will clarify how that structure works. Of course, there is no single agreed-upon way to structure a screenplay, but many theorists and gurus have converged on the following traits:[10]

1. In the first act, an inciting incident breaks the protagonist's routine and prompts the protagonist to lock onto a specific conflict.
2. In the second act, the protagonist struggles to accomplish the goal. At the midpoint, the protagonist may experience a temporary triumph or some other turning point.
3. At the end of the second act, the protagonist often experiences a darkest moment, momentarily giving up the struggle.
4. In the third act, a twist gets the protagonist back on track, leading to a climax where the protagonist accomplishes the overall goal.

Kloves structures the dementor plot along these lines. In the first act Harry's routine trip to Hogwarts is disrupted when he confronts the dementors; at the school he realizes that he might have to face his fears again when Dumbledore warns him that the dementors will be patrolling the grounds. A few minutes later the film fades to black on an image of the dementors flying by. This fade-out, which occurs roughly twenty-nine minutes into the film, marks the end of the first act. The first act has generated a question that will structure the rest of the film: Will Harry be able to overcome the dementors when he inevitably meets them again? The long second act returns to this question several times. In Defense Against the Dark Arts class, taught by Professor Lupin, Harry confronts a dementor (actually a boggart that has taken on the shape of Harry's deepest fears).[11] During the film's only Quidditch match, a real dementor causes Harry to fall off his broom. After the winter break Lupin uses a boggart to teach Harry how he can use the Patronus charm to defeat the dementor. Harry fails at first but tries again and succeeds. I take the Patronus lesson, which happens about 70 minutes into the film, to be the movie's midpoint.[12] The scene accomplishes two structural goals. On the level of questions and answers, the scene sharpens the presiding question: Will Harry be able to master the Patronus charm to overcome the dementors? On the level of hopes and fears, the scene provides a high point marking the middle of Harry's journey—after several previous failures, Harry has finally defeated a dementor.[13] This high point provides a reason to hope, but it is not yet a story-ending triumph. Because the dementor was just a boggart, Harry has not accomplished his goal yet. The film then drops the dementor storyline for nearly half an hour, only to bring the dementors back forcefully for the darkest moment that ends the long second act. In screenwriting terms, a *darkest moment* is a scene, roughly three-quarters of the way through the film, in which the protagonist seems to have lost the battle not just momentarily but decisively.[14] Here, Harry confronts dozens of dementors, and he fails to defeat them. He is rescued only by an apparent *deus ex machina*: the mysterious person who casts the Patronus charm from across the lake. The act ends with another fade to black, as Harry passes out. Notice how the darkest moment at the end of the second act has inverted the midpoint. The midpoint gave us reason to hope that Harry would succeed; the darkest moment makes it appear that Harry has failed miserably. In canonically structured scripts, the darkest moment is followed by a third-act twist—some unexpected event that gets the protagonist back on track.[15] Hermione's Time Turner is a classic third-act twist, providing Harry a final chance to accomplish his goal. A bit after the two-hour mark, Harry conjures the Patronus charm again, this time triumphantly. The result is a complete storyline with a classic structure. In the following list, notice how each step in the progression works in terms of questions, answers, hopes, and fears.

1. The first act poses a question based in fear: Will Harry overcome the dementors?
2. The midpoint sharpens the question: Will Harry use the Patronus charm to overcome the dementors? There is reason to hope because he appears to have mastered the charm.
3. The darkest moment provides a false answer that fulfills our fears. No, Harry will fail to overcome the dementors because he cannot cast a successful Patronus charm. (Or so it seems.)
4. The climax provides a definitive answer that fulfills our hopes. Yes, he will succeed in defeating the dementors, and he will do so by successfully casting the Patronus charm.

This structure is so solid that Kloves can layer other structures on top of it, even when they are less canonical. In interviews Kloves has insisted that he prefers character to plot, and many of his other script choices bring character to the fore.[16] The Sirius plot links causally to the dementors plot, but its structure highlights the internal shifts in Harry's moral views rather than the active shifts in his conjuring prowess. Harry faces a clear problem—Sirius Black wants to kill him—but he does not lock onto this conflict until late in the story. In the first act Harry

explicitly adopts a passive position. Mr. Weasley asks Harry to
assure him that he will not chase after Black, and Harry replies
(in dialogue taken straight from the book), "Why would I go
looking for someone who wants to kill me?"[17] Halfway through
the film Harry has reversed his position; he tells Hermione, "I
hope he finds me. . . . When he does, I'm going to kill him."[18]
Now he has a more active goal, but it is a troubling one that
he must abandon. If this is the midpoint of the Sirius subplot,
then it contrasts with the midpoint of the dementors plot in
an important way. The midpoint of the dementors plot is an
"up" moment, amplifying the hope that Harry will accomplish
his goal. The midpoint of the Sirius plot is a "down" moment,
amplifying the fear that Harry will give in to his worst instincts
and become a killer like Sirius himself. The remainder of this
plot must set Harry back on a positive trajectory. In the crucial
Shrieking Shack scene, Harry has the opportunity to kill Sirius,
but he chooses not to do so, with the help of some moral guidance from Hermione and Lupin. After Peter Pettigrew's guilt is
revealed, Harry prevents Sirius from becoming the killer he has
long believed him to be and instead agrees to hand Peter over
to the dementors to await their dark justice. Given the brutality
of the wizarding world's prison system, the morality of this lat-
est choice is ambivalent at best: Harry has chosen institution-
alized torture over personal murder. The time-travel plot gives
Harry a chance to reverse this flawed decision, as well. Rather
than aid the dementors, he rescues a prisoner (Sirius) from
their grasp. Again, the storyline follows a pattern of reversals:

1. Harry wants to avoid getting killed by Sirius—a
   passive but worthy goal.
2. Then Harry wants to kill Sirius—an active but
   unworthy goal.

3. Then Harry wants to let the dementors punish Peter—a passive goal of dubious worth.
4. Finally, Harry wants to rescue Sirius from the dementors—an active, worthy goal.

In this storyline Harry does not become an active hero with a worthy goal until the end. The delayed agency of the Sirius plot echoes that of the Buckbeak subplot. Harry spends much of the film passively hoping that the Ministry will not execute Buckbeak; only in the end does he actively work with the more socially conscious Hermione to defy institutional authority and rescue the hippogriff.

All of this suggests that Harry emerges as the canonical hero in the third act, but even that assessment overstates the case. In his most daring structural decision, Kloves gives the bulk of the third act to Hermione, who performs the role of the active protagonist while Harry follows along in confusion. Although Harry becomes a last-second hero, this shift toward Hermione offers the pleasures of a classic suspense scenario: a strong and determined character (in this case Hermione) races, quite literally, against the ticking of the clock. The screenplay adjusts and amplifies little details from the book to make Hermione more active.[19] In the book's Shrieking Shack scene, it is Ron who tells Sirius, "If you want to kill Harry, you'll have to kill us, too!"[20] The screenplay gives the line to Hermione.[21] In the book it is Harry who figures out that Dumbledore intends for them to rescue the doomed hippogriff: "And then it hit him. 'Hermione, we're going to save Buckbeak!'"[22] In the screenplay Hermione makes the connection, and Harry remains a step behind: "HARRY: Buckbeak? But . . . how will saving Buckbeak help Sirius?"[23] In the book

Hermione does not throw a stone to alert her past self to leave Hagrid's cabin, and she does not produce a wolf call to rescue Harry from the werewolf. In the screenplay she does both. ("HARRY: What are you doing? HERMIONE: Saving your life!")[24] In the book Hermione is not present for the successful casting of the Patronus charm.[25] In the screenplay her words push Harry toward the climactic revelation. The spell itself belongs to Harry alone; he becomes the hero, at last.[26] But the surprise is even more surprising because he has been so passive for the past twenty minutes.

A VERY TELLABLE STORY

This analysis of the screenplay's structure might make it seem like Kloves was following a rigorous template, as if he were an over-eager reader of Syd Field.[27] However, his decisions make sense for other reasons, regardless of which structural model he may subscribe to. Within narrative theory, one useful topic of discussion (often overlooked in film narratology) concerns a story's "tellability." A story might meet the strictest definition of narrative—for instance, it might represent a set of events connected by cause and effect—and yet seem strangely pointless. Quite apart from defining whether a story is or is not a narrative, a theorist of tellability might ask what makes a given narrative seem worth recounting in the first place. The answer is partly dependent on context: a story about the weather might lack a point if the listener is sitting comfortably inside, but it might be very worth telling if the listener is standing outside without an umbrella. For a commercial film aimed at a mass audience, the primary point might lie simply in the story's ability to generate interest and emotion. As Marie-Laure Ryan explains, "A theory of tellability implicitly regards a plot as a sequence of peaks and valleys, and seeks out the formulae for building up the peaks."[28] The relevance for the *Harry Potter* series seems clear. Rowling writes exceptionally tellable stories that feature extraordinarily intense peaks and valleys.

Ryan proposes four traits that may make a story more tellable: *semantic opposition, semantic parallelism, functional polyvalence*, and a particular feature that she calls the diversification of *virtual embedded narratives.*[29] In both novel and screenplay forms, *Prisoner of Azkaban* abounds in all four traits.

1. Semantic opposition. Narrative theorists from the time of Aristotle have noted that stories often contain powerful reversals of fortune in which success becomes failure or vice versa. In *Prisoner of Azkaban* everything seems to be going well after the Shrieking Shack scene: Harry has apprehended Peter Pettigrew, the man who betrayed his parents, and he has done so with the help of two father figures, Remus Lupin and Sirius Black. Then the moon comes out, and a narrative peak becomes a valley instantaneously. Lupin turns into a werewolf, Pettigrew escapes, and Sirius is attacked by dementors. The time-travel sequence reverses the reversal, allowing Harry to rescue Sirius from the dementors. The valley becomes a peak once more. Such semantic oppositions also structure Harry's changing goals. At first Harry has no intention of confronting Sirius. Reversal: Harry wants to kill Sirius. Double reversal: Harry wants to save Sirius.

2. Semantic parallelism. From the standpoint of tellability theory, stringing two events together via causality is not always enough to make the resulting story worth telling. The events are more interesting when they have some other

sort of relationship, whether one of reversal or repetition. *Prisoner of Azkaban* turns several characters into doubles—or triples—of one another. Lupin, Sirius, and James are all father figures—one a metaphorical father, one a godfather, one a biological father. Sirius and Peter are both suspected of betraying Harry's parents—one falsely, the other correctly. Lupin, Sirius, and Peter all can turn into animals—a wolf, a dog, and a rat. Other doubles include Fred and George Weasley and Harry and Voldemort.[30] As a children's film, *Prisoner of Azkaban* makes its parallels very clear, as when Hermione comments via dialogue that saving Buckbeak is similar to saving Sirius.

3. Functional polyvalence. Ryan uses this term to describe moments that resolve particular narrative problems in an elegant way.[31] For instance, the revelation that Scabbers is Peter Pettigrew accomplishes several storytelling goals in one stroke. It answers the question of why Scabbers has been disappearing. It explains why Sirius broke out of Azkaban—not to kill Harry, but to kill Peter. It proves that Lupin is worthy of Harry's trust even if he is a friend of Sirius. And it sets the stage for Harry to make his final moral choice about whether or not to allow Sirius and Lupin to kill Peter. Similarly, the time-travel sequence answers a lingering question (Why has Hermione been appearing in the middle of class?) while preparing for the resolution of almost all the major storylines.

4. Virtual embedded narratives. This concept is Ryan's crucial contribution to tellability theory, and it is particularly relevant to the *Harry Potter* series. Ryan defines embedded narratives as "the story-like constructs contained in the private worlds of characters."[32] For instance, when a character plans to accomplish a goal, the accomplishment of the goal becomes a "virtual event." It exists in the mind of the character,

whether the character actually accomplishes the goal or not. As such, it shapes the reader's understanding of the events that do occur. The category is meant to be expansive. Hopes, fears, false beliefs, accurate beliefs, impossible dreams, lingering suspicions—all of these states produce their own embedded narratives, some of which will be actualized, some of which will not. Encountering a narrative involves more than just keeping track of the causal chain; it involves keeping track of the events that do happen in light of all the events that the characters thought would happen—or could happen or should happen.

Having made this distinction, Ryan offers a bold proposal: "The aesthetic appeal of a plot is a function of the richness and variety of the domain of the virtual, as it is surveyed and made accessible by those private embedded narratives."[33] Put simply, the more virtual events a story has, the more tellable the story becomes. When everyone in the story-world agrees on what events have happened, what events will happen, and what events should happen, then the story lacks interest and risk. A story becomes more engaging when one character wants (or expects or fears) one thing, and another character wants (or expects or fears) something else.

I do not know if Ryan's theory of tellability is applicable to all narratives. As noted, the point of a story varies in context; in some contexts a thoroughly predictable narrative might prove to be perfectly tellable. But the theory seems ideal for an analysis of *Prisoner of Azkaban*, a highly tellable story that multiplies its embedded narratives to an extraordinary degree. Consider this single line of dialogue spoken by Mr. Weasley to Harry in the Leaky Cauldron: "I want you to swear that—whatever you might hear—you won't go looking for Black." Mr. Weasley imagines a world where Harry looks for Black. He imagines various alternative versions of that world, where Harry looks for Black based on assorted things he has heard. And then he imagines a world where Harry does not go looking for Black, precisely because he—Mr. Weasley—has intervened by securing a promise from Harry. When, halfway through the movie, Harry announces that he will kill Black if he gets the chance, the scene derives additional emotional power because the *virtual world* that Mr. Weasley tried to prevent has now come to be. At the same time, Harry's announcement opens up a new embedded narrative, whereby Harry imagines killing his godfather. This darker turn almost comes to pass, but it does not for a reason that is equally tied to virtual events—Harry's false embedded narrative about the past (that Black betrayed his parents) gets replaced by a true embedded narrative about the past (that Pettigrew betrayed his parents).

Kloves sharpens Rowling's embedded narratives by foregrounding the characters' wants and needs in the film's dialogue, as in these lines, taken from various scenes:

HAGRID (regarding Buckbeak): Who wants to come say hello?

NEVILLE (regarding his grandmother): I don't want the boggart to turn into her, either.

McGONAGALL (regarding Sirius): Now he wants to finish what he started.

HERMIONE (to Sirius): If you want to kill Harry, you'll have to kill us, too!

HARRY (to Sirius): I don't reckon my father'd want his best friends to become killers.

HERMIONE (about Dumbledore): Clearly something happened he wants us to change.

HARRY (to Sirius): I want to go with you.

LUPIN (after he is sacked): Parents will not want a—
      someone like me—teaching their children.[34]

Each time a character talks about wants (or hopes or fears), an
embedded narrative opens up, creating a contrast between the
virtual and the actual. These embedded narratives make the
story more tellable by suggesting all the ways that the world
could be different.

MANAGING POINT OF VIEW

To make sense of these embedded narratives, the viewer
must take multiple characters' perspectives (beliefs, hopes,
attitudes) into account. However, the screenplay does not
slip from Harry to Hermione to Sirius to Snape. With a few
notable exceptions, Kloves's screenplay follows the restrictive
pattern laid down in Rowling's book: Harry must appear in
every scene.

Such an approach was by no means automatic. *Order of the
Phoenix*, based on the fifth book in the series and the only film
in the series not scripted by Kloves, breaks from the book's
rigorously focalized approach several times, showing many
events that Harry does not witness: Neville Longbottom dis-
covering the Room of Requirement, Bellatrix Lestrange escaping from Azkaban, Argus Filch taking the paintings off
the walls.[35] These additions add suspense, excitement, and
humor, but they do so at a cost: the spectator loses the sense
of attachment to Harry's fallible, limited perspective on the
wizarding world. *Prisoner of Azkaban*'s more focused approach
involves some sacrifices, too: there is no dash of excitement

from an added prison escape scene, no uptick in suspense from a cutaway to Lupin staring at the full moon. But the gain is considerable, amplifying the surprises that Rowling has constructed so deftly. While offering just enough hints along the way to ensure that viewers do not feel cheated, the film refuses to reveal the full truth about Sirius, Scabbers, and Lupin until Harry learns it himself in the Shrieking Shack late in the film.

The focused approach allows the filmmakers to develop one of the film's central themes: Harry's search for a father figure. Discussing his working relationship with Kloves, Cuarón explained, "It's all about eliminating redundancies. We decided to be precise about what our theme was and then cut away anything that didn't follow in that direction."[36] This philosophy explains some of the eliminations mentioned above—the cuts of book scenes involving Quidditch and Crookshanks—but it also explains the addition of two quiet scenes wherein Harry learns about his connection to his parents. In the first, Lupin describes the kindness of Harry's mother and the rebelliousness of Harry's father, and he assures Harry that he is more like them than he knows.[37] In the second, Sirius tells Harry how moved he is to see that Harry resembles his parents physically. A verbal motif connects the two scenes; both Lupin and Sirius tell Harry that he has his mother's eyes.[38] The comparable Sirius scene from the book is much less sentimental—and, in my view, less moving. Sirius is rushing to escape; he only has time to say, "You are—truly your father's son, Harry."[39] To be sure, the credit for these scenes does not belong solely to Kloves. By the time he wrote this screenplay, Rowling had released *Order of the Phoenix*, and the dialogue in these scenes points ahead to future developments she had already devised. Harry will later grow tired of people telling him he has his mother's eyes, and Sirius's determination to compare Harry to his father will turn out to be a major flaw in Sirius's character. While the film version of *Prisoner of Azkaban* does depart from the book, it does so to situate the story more deeply within the unfolding character arcs of the larger series.

The screenplay's adherence to the focalization principle is not perfect. For the freeing of Sirius, the script recommends cross-cutting between Hermione casting the spell and Snape and Fudge racing to stop her.[40] But the finished film rejects this violation and keeps the focus on Hermione and Harry instead. Another violation does make it into the finished film, and the film is all the better for it. This violation involves various shots of scenery outside of Hogwarts. Several scenes in the film show such outside views even though Harry is going about his business within Hogwarts's walls. At the most basic level, these scenes reinforce the dementor plot by reminding us that the foul creatures are still stalking the school's grounds. More generally, the scenes evoke the passage of time by showing the Whomping Willow in various stages of seasonal transformation—with its leaves, without its leaves, covered in snow, and beginning to bloom again. The passage of time seems unavoidable and absolute—a perfect metaphor for a film about growing up and the perfect foil for a movie with a big plot twist about time travel.

THE STORY WITHIN THE SERIES

Kloves addressed an additional challenge that most adapters never need to face—the challenge of fitting each film into a still-unfolding series. Recent works by narrative theorists, philosophers, and critics have called attention to the unique dynamics of serial narratives. As philosopher Andrew McGonigal defines the term, a work of serial fiction is one that unfolds over the course of several distinct episodes, such as a prime-time dramatic television show, a run of Sherlock Holmes stories, or a major studio movie with one or more sequels. The production and reception of such fictions are "(i) connected in an interesting way to distinct, relevantly discontinuous episodes or instalments that are (ii) appropriately construable as taking place in a single fictional world."[41] Whereas a self-standing film traditionally tells a complete story in around two hours, serial fictions often leave a dangling storyline to be picked up by future instalments of the series. Television has long illustrated how the category of serial fiction covers a vast spectrum of possibilities, including the following: soap operas that run for decades, favoring seriality over narrative closure; crime shows that develop and resolve a single mystery per episode, favoring episodic unity over serial engagement; and miniseries, which stretch a single story over several episodes, all leading toward an ending carefully scripted in advance.[42] Even within a single series the balance might shift from episode to episode, featuring some episodes that function as stand-alone units and others that function as contributions to long-running arcs.

The *Harry Potter* franchise artfully balances the serial ambition to stretch the story over eight films (based on seven books) with the episodic imperative to make each movie satisfying on its own. If my analysis so far has focused on *Prisoner of Azkaban*'s achievements as a stand-alone film, it is partly because I see the movie as the most episodic entry in the series. Taken as a whole, the series' most important plots include the Voldemort plot and the romance plots, but they make little progress here. The film places much more emphasis on the Lupin storyline—that is, the story about the Defense Against the Dark Arts teacher, which is always an episodic storyline that reaches a resolution at the end of each installment. Even the movie's big twist—the Time Turner—turns out to be an episodic feature, not a serial one, as this too-powerful tool never gets used in a meaningful way again until the production of the stage play *Harry Potter and the Cursed Child*.[43] These traits make *Prisoner of Azkaban* seem like a magical version of the police procedural *Law & Order*, featuring Hermione as the detective who solves the case of the week.

That said, *Prisoner of Azkaban* remains a part of a series, and its seriality does add a great deal of enjoyment and richness to its narrative. In the previous two entries, Hagrid was something of an outcast, having been expelled from Hogwarts many years earlier because of a false accusation. This background makes it all the more satisfying when we learn that Hagrid has won a promotion in *Prisoner of Azkaban*—and all the more worrisome when Draco threatens to have Hagrid fired. In the previous two entries, Harry has suffered neglect and abuse at the hands of the Dursleys. This background makes it all the more understandable when Harry takes revenge on Aunt Marge. These examples both point backward in the story-world, but the movie also points forward, leaving several dangling questions for subsequent films to address: Will Harry accomplish his goal of living with his newfound godfather? How exactly will Peter aid Voldemort in his return? These questions maintain suspense, even for viewers who come into the film knowing the story from the book.

Cuarón's film came out in 2004, a year after *Order of the Phoenix* had been released as the fifth book. Dedicated readers found themselves in the interesting position of knowing some of the story's future outcomes, but not all of them. They could immerse themselves in the world of the film but also interpret the film in light of the fifth book's revelations. And yet the larger scheme was still unfolding. As literary scholar Beatrice Groves explains, the seven-book series as a whole would eventually form a "chiastic" pattern, "in which events are repeated in inverse order."[44] In other words, book seven would echo book one, book six would echo book two, and book five would echo book three, with book four serving as a pivot point. These echoes do not simply replay earlier scenes; they revise them in a darker and more serious direction. Comparing *Prisoner of Azkaban* to *Order of the Phoenix* makes the earlier book seem surprisingly upbeat. In the former book Harry rescues Sirius. In the latter Voldemort tricks Harry into thinking that he needs to rescue Sirius again, but the attempted rescue leads to Sirius's death. In the former book the new Defense Against the Dark Arts teacher is the best teacher Harry has ever had. In the latter the new Defense Against the Dark Arts teacher is the worst. In the former Harry benefits from the love and support of Dumbledore. In the latter Dumbledore deliberately ignores Harry for hundreds of pages. In the former Harry consistently defends his father from Snape's accusations. In the latter he learns that Snape's accusations were true. All of these inversions develop the same idea. In the third book Harry venerates his father figures. In the fifth he distrusts them, questions them, and loses them.[45]

Camera, Perspective, and Point of View

When *Prisoner of Azkaban* was released, several critics pronounced it the best of the series so far—a judgment that many critics have echoed in recent years, even after the series ended in 2011.[1] Not surprisingly, director Alfonso Cuarón has received much of the credit, both for his willingness to depart from the book's particulars without losing its spirit and for his ability to give the film a fresh visual style. These same critics often note that the film is darker than its predecessors—literally, with its rich, black shadows, but also thematically, with its shift from childhood to adolescence. There is some truth to this point about darkness, but the point can be taken too far; it is still a PG-rated movie with wizards and witches, hippogriffs and Hufflepuffs. For all its dramatic intensity, we should not forget that among its most admirable features are its brisk pace and its sense of humor, both of which do great justice to Rowling's wit.

As Cuarón scholar Deborah Shaw points out, the director's career has alternated between "director-for-hire" projects and more personal works that self-consciously draw on his carefully constructed identity as an auteur.[2] Although *Prisoner of Azkaban* is located firmly in the former camp, Cuarón still manages to pursue longstanding interests. One of these interests is point of view. His previous film, the sex-drenched road film *Y Tu Mamá También*, had experimented with an omniscient (but strategically uncommunicative) narrator who interrupts the action to deliver dry commentary about Mexican politics and proleptic remarks about events that will happen to the characters in the future. *Prisoner of Azbakan* pushes these experiments in another direction, using carefully designed camerawork to explore variations on the theme of point of view while working in a largely focalized framework. This tactic—narrowing the film's range down to a single character—would inform *Children of Men* (2006) and *Gravity* (2013), as well.

If we consider *Prisoner of Azkaban* at the level of its scene-by-scene construction, we see that the film appears to be focalized through Harry. However, at the level of its shot-by-shot construction, the film seems less closely tied to Harry's range of knowledge. Aside from a few POV shots, the camera usually shows Harry from the outside—sometimes in the manner of a detached observer, but more often expressively, moving in ways that evoke Harry's emotions. As the film progresses, it loosens its exclusive attachment to Harry and incorporates the perspectives of other characters—most notably Hermione. Crucially, Cuarón's visual strategy here *expands* rather than shifts. It is not that the perspective switches from Harry to Hermione; it is that the film's cinematic point of view grows more inclusive, taking in Hermione's perspective as well as Harry's. As scholar Vera Cuntz-Leng explains, "In contrast to the novels, the film adaptations allow a certain freedom from Harry's fixed perspective. . . . The process of reception is no longer moderated by the animosities and sympathies of the protagonist."[3] By asking viewers to compare how Harry and Hermione experience events, the film implicitly calls on its viewers to consider the characters' competing conceptions of agency and time.

In previous sections I have helped myself to the narratological terms focalization and filter, which nicely capture the way that the book narrates story events only when Harry encounters them, even though he does not narrate the books. However, my analysis of the film's shifting framing strategies requires a more flexible term. Following the literary theorist Meir Sternberg, I will use the term *perspectival motivation*.[4] The theory of motivation explains how readers or spectators make sense of unexpected features in the work and how a text may organize those features to shape the sense-making process. One relevant contrast is between *functional* motivation and *fictional* motivation. In the former (also known as rhetorical motivation), a spectator makes sense of a textual feature by appealing to means-end logic: perhaps the film is concealing a key piece of information in order to maximize curiosity. In the latter (also known as mimetic motivation), a spectator appeals to reasons within the story-world: perhaps the key piece of information is hidden behind a doorway or magically invisible. Fictional motivation works within functional motivation. A film may depict a world filled with locked doors and invisibility cloaks precisely to conceal information and maximize curiosity. Within the category of fictional motivation, an unusual feature may be motivated *existentially* or *perspectivally*. Suppose a movie shifts from an event in the present to an event in the past. If the movie in question is science fiction or fantasy, the shift in chronology might be motivated existentially by appealing to the ontology of the fictional world: perhaps this world allows time travel. If the movie is a psychological drama, the shift in chronology might be motivated perspectivally by appealing to the mediation of a character's experience: perhaps a character is remembering the past. (Or the shift in chronology might lack fictional motivation altogether. The movie might simply cut to the past for functional or rhetorical reasons without giving any reason in the story-world.) As a fantasy film with an interest in character psychology, *Prisoner of Azkaban* does both. Sometimes we hear events from the past because Harry is remembering the sound of those events in the present (appealing to perspectival motivation); sometimes we observe events from the past because Harry and Hermione have traveled back in time to reenact them (appealing to existential motivation).

This theory of motivation also explains aspects of the film's camerawork and framing. This point may seem surprising. In many films framing simply does not require fictional motivation, whether existential or perspectival.[5] There is no camera in the fictional world, and the camera's placement simply registers as a functional storytelling device, creating patterns of revelation and concealment to produce thematic and emotional effects. That said, there is at least one class of camera angles that does appeal to fictional motivation: POV shots, where the angle, height, and position of the camera serve to represent a character's optical experience. Expanding the category, some shots seem to be mediated or inflected by character subjectivity, even when they are not literal POV shots. Perhaps the low angle of a shot figuratively expresses a character's attitude of wonder toward an unfolding event; perhaps the rapid speed of a dolly movement expresses a character's confusion or delight or despair. The philosopher George M. Wilson has called this approach "indirect or reflected subjectivity." In this mode, he writes, "properties of the way in which the fictional world looks to us on the screen stand in for properties of the way in which that world is experienced by the character."[6] Framing, angle, and movement are properties of the film's discourse, not of the film's story-world, but in the right contexts they may evoke a character's emotion or awareness or attention or confusion. Here it can be useful to think of perspectival motivation as an appeal to perspectival *understanding*, enabling spectators to make sense of textual details by reading them as inflected by character experience. Once we suppose that a shot may evoke a character's perspective in all of its many aspects, the next step is to grant that a shot may appeal to the viewer's understanding of multiple perspectives—in succession or even simultaneously. *Prisoner of Azkaban* is a veritable compendium of perspectival possibilities. Remarkably, the resulting film is never confusing: on the existential level it is easy to understand what is happening where and when, even during the potentially confusing time-travel sequence. Meanwhile, the camerawork consistently appeals to perspectival understanding, often in multiple ways at once.

AMPLIFIED POV SHOTS

Cuarón's longtime collaborator Emmanuel "Chivo" Lubezki was unavailable to shoot the film; the job of cinematographer went to Michael Seresin, a New Zealand–born director of photography (DP) best known for his work with British director Alan Parker. Together, Cuarón and Seresin opted to move the camera in almost every shot, relying on dollies, cranes, Steadicams, handheld work, and computer-generated (CG) camerawork to do so.

Some of these resulting shots are unambiguously POV shots,

as in the scene in which Harry eavesdrops on the conversation at Madame Rosmerta's, where handheld camerawork and a digitally added fabric effect represent Harry's POV as he looks through an invisibility cloak. Harry's POV seems bumpy and obscured; it is appropriate that he is learning an unsettling truth (which will, in the end, turn out to be false). Later, in the Whomping Willow scene, the camerawork undercuts the perceptive power of Harry's POV again. As the tree smashes Harry to the ground, his glasses fall off. The film cuts to his POV, and everything is out of focus. By contrast, Hermione's POV looks sharp, even though the tree is hurling her through the sky. The immediate effect is immersive and experiential, giving us an affective understanding of what Harry and Hermione are feeling in this chaotic moment. But the technique also provides a metacommentary, as if Cuarón were using the blurry POV shot to expose Harry's perspective as limited and confused.

Such literal POV shots are actually somewhat rare in the film. More often, camera movement creates what I call amplified POV shots, representing what Harry sees with an added evocation of what he feels.[7] An early scene offers a clear example. After transforming the Thatcheresque Aunt Marge into a balloon, Harry leaves the Dursley residence and sits on a curb with his suitcase. The next several shots form a recurring pattern as Harry looks around at his increasingly menacing surroundings. First Harry looks up; cut to a low-angle shot of the blinking streetlight above him (figures 1 and 2). Then Harry looks back; cut to shots of the eerily deserted playground behind him. And then Harry looks forward; cut to a shot of the menacing black dog emerging to face him. In the corresponding scene from the book, Rowling's prose filters its descriptions through Harry's perceptions: "Harry saw, quite distinctly, the hulking outline of something very big, with wide, gleaming eyes."[8] The shot progression accomplishes a similar effect, depicting Harry's worried expression from the outside and then depicting the frightful forms that he sees, as if from the inside.

Figure 1.   Waiting for the bus, Harry looks up . . .

Figure 2.   . . . and sees a blinking streetlamp.

On closer inspection, though, the POV shots cannot be literal representations of Harry's optical perceptions. The POV shot of the streetlight is craning up, even though Harry is sitting still, and the POV shots of the black dog are moving forward, even though Harry remains in one place. In between, the shots of the playground form a small montage, depicting the empty structures from a variety of angles, none of which Harry occupies. Adhering to a strict definition of the technique, one might refuse to count these shots as POV shots altogether. But the framework of perspectival motivation includes all of these shots. The perspective of each shot (in the narrowly spatial sense of the term) makes more sense when one interprets the composition according to the logic of Harry's perspective (in the experiential sense of the term). Not only do the shots show what Harry sees, they do so in a way that evokes his experience of these disturbing sights. The slow movements suggest the build-up of Harry's anxiety; the increasing proximity to the dog suggests the perceived imminence of the threat. Even the shots of Harry himself appeal to perspectival understanding by suggesting the presence of some malevolent force circling the hero. Harry looks up toward the streetlight, and the camera cranes up to look down on him from above. In the story-world his fears implicitly endow the streetlamp with a kind of consciousness, as if it were blinking not because of a malfunction but to threaten him. When the camera swings over Harry, it momentarily adopts the streetlamp's spatial perspective. By evoking the lamp's "point of view" (looking down ominously on Harry), the positioning endows the lamp with the malevolent consciousness that Harry momentarily suspects that it may have. Later, when the camera wanders through the playground, its menacing movements evoke the prowl of some evil spirit—not because an evil spirit is really there but because Harry temporarily fears such ominous possibilities.

This suspenseful scene plants an idea that will soon become a theme: the idea of the omen. Harry takes these sights—the blinking streetlamp, the revolving merry-go-round, the snarling black dog—as premonitions of doom. Professor Trelawney eventually will give a name to the dog—the Grim— but the scene shows that Harry is prone to feelings of foreboding already. The scene's slow-moving dolly and crane shots thereby provide insight into Harry's character, hinting that Harry may be overly obsessed with his own fate, as if he cannot help being pulled toward images of death. In this way the camerawork opens up some distance between the movie's cinematic point of view and Harry's perspective. The cinematic point of view (that is, its rhetorical orientation) subtly relativizes Harry's outlook even when it represents events through his eyes.

The film contains several other POV shots, and almost all of them are amplified similarly by camera movements that add a psychological dimension to the literal representation of optical experience. The camera rarely occupies Harry's exact position in space for long; instead, it dollies toward (or cranes up to or arcs around) the subject of his attention, whether the subject is the *Monster Book of Monsters* chomping under the bed or the ever-changing Marauder's Map. Rather than disqualify the shots as POV shots, these movements appeal to perspectival understanding all the more. Understanding Harry's perspective requires that we understand more than just what he sees; we also must understand what he feels, what he hopes, what he believes, and sometimes even what he should be seeing but fails to notice.

INSIDE OUT

This more expansive conception of perspectival understanding helps make sense of Cuarón's seemingly paradoxical claim that the film is told from Harry's point of view even though it only occasionally looks through his eyes. The bulk of the film consists of external shots—shots of Harry seen from the outside—but such external views repeatedly appeal to perspectival understanding in its broadest sense, including all aspects of a character's experience. For instance, consider the scene when Harry overhears Dumbledore and Snape talking about Sirius's infiltration of Hogwarts. In the book Rowling takes special care to describe only what Harry can see and hear. At the start of the scene, Harry keeps his eyes closed because he is pretending to be asleep, and Rowling's prose sticks closely to Harry's aural perceptions: "Harry heard the door of the hall creak open again, and more footsteps. 'Headmaster?' It was Snape. Harry kept quite still, listening hard."[9] Rather than write that Snape opens the door and enters the hall, Rowling describes the sounds without naming Snape right away, acknowledging that Harry cannot see who has opened the door. The word "Snape" appears only after Harry has identified the teacher by the sound of his voice. Similarly, Rowling describes crucial visual details only later in the scene, after Harry sneaks a peek: "Harry opened his eyes a fraction and squinted up to where they stood; Dumbledore's back was to him, but he could see Percy's face, rapt with attention, and Snape's profile, which looked angry."[10] The literary focalization remains consistent. Rather than state that Snape is angry, Rowling writes that Snape "looked" angry, thereby providing access to Snape's emotions only through the filter of what Harry can observe from his outward appearance.

In Cuarón's film the scene unfolds differently, showing aspects of the scene that Harry cannot possibly perceive. The camera starts high above the Great Hall; Dumbledore and

Snape appear in extreme long shot, and Harry is nowhere to be seen. Then the camera cranes down and reveals Harry with his eyes open, lying in the foreground of the shot and looking away from the teachers. A rack focus ensures that Harry's facial expression is visible; Dumbledore and Snape look soft in the background (figure 3). The point of the shot is to show what Harry does *not* see. He cannot see Dumbledore and Snape behind him, he cannot see Filch carrying a lamp in the deep background, he cannot see all the other students in their blankets, and of course he cannot see himself. But the representation of what a character *could* see but *does not* see still refers to the character's perspective, albeit obliquely. Part of the shot's meaning lies in its power to suggest certain hypotheticals: Harry could see Dumbledore if he turned around, and Snape could see Harry if he stepped forward a few feet. In the book passage Rowling emphasizes Harry's deficient visual awareness of the events around him by restricting her prose to aural details. Cuarón emphasizes Harry's deficient visual awareness by showing those events clearly and then revealing Harry's exact position in space so we can understand that he cannot quite see them.

Figure 3.   The camera cranes down to reveal that Harry is not sleeping.

With its external view, the shot translates certain effects of Rowling's prose into visual terms. Readers of the book must make inferences from outward behavior to understand certain thoughts and attitudes of Snape and Dumbledore—namely, Snape's malevolent intention to undercut Dumbledore's trust in Lupin and Dumbledore's benevolent intention to ignore Snape's aspersions. Similarly, the film relies on the expert performances of Alan Rickman and Michael Gambon to convey those ideas via their characters' outward behavior. If the film had consisted of an unending series of POV shots from Harry's perspective, then it would have failed to capture the nuances of the book's approach, which privileges Harry's perspective without adopting his narrative voice.

The two surrounding shots complicate the picture even more. Just prior to this shot, the film has shown the dementors patrolling the grounds; in the background the lights dim in the Great Hall. Although Harry is, in a very loose sense of the word, "in" the shot (since he is in the Great Hall, which is prominently placed in the composition), the example stretches the principle of focalization to the breaking point. Directly after the shot of Harry pretending to be asleep, the film cuts to a low-angle shot of Dumbledore and Snape as Dumbledore delivers a poetic monologue about dreaming. The camera cranes up past the two teachers to focus on the enchanted ceiling above (figure 4). At first the shot represents what Harry *would* see if he turned around. Then the camera moves toward Dumbledore, who delivers his monologue while looking down toward Harry. The expression on the headmaster's face suggests that he knows full well that Harry is awake; the monologue about the value of dreams seems meant for Harry, not for Snape. When the camera moves past the teachers to frame the starlit ceiling above them, the film bypasses the characters altogether to show what no one but the audience sees. Yet even this image is not entirely disconnected from character consciousness; abstractly, the movement evokes the deeper meaning of Dumbledore's speech. Just as the headmaster is advising Harry to enjoy the moments of wonder that dreams can bring, the framing of the sky offers viewers a brief moment to delight in all the wonders that digital cinema can provide.

Figure 4.   A low-angle shot reveals what Harry does not see.

Cuarón's film generally remains within Harry's range of awareness, but *awareness* is a very broad term. One can be aware of something without perceiving it directly; Harry is aware that Dumbledore and Snape are behind him, even if he does not turn to see them. For that matter, Harry is aware that dementors are patrolling the grounds, even though he could not possibly see them, as they are outside and he is inside. The film's restricted range feels very different from the restricted range of the novel—partly because it defines awareness so loosely and partly because film, as a visual medium, offers far more textural detail than a medium-sized book could provide. The previously quoted passage in *Prisoner of Azkaban* contains a string of carefully selected words that describe only those aspects of Dumbledore, Snape, and the Great Hall that Harry actively notices and hears. The corresponding scene in Cuarón's film loosens Rowling's focalization to draw subtle distinctions between different kinds of perceptual experiences, showing what Harry is only dimly aware of (the dementors flying outside the Hall), what Harry is paying attention to even though he cannot turn his head to see it (the conversation between Dumbledore and Snape), and what he might be able to appreciate if he was not so worried about everything else (the enchanted ceiling, so evocative of the dreams that Dumbledore extols). Cuarón's interest in Harry's perspective extends well beyond Harry's immediate perceptions to take in a range of nuances and variations: dim awareness, active concentration, possible perceptions, and even missed opportunities.

MULTIPLE PERSPECTIVES

So is the film told from Harry's point of view or not? The question is puzzling and perhaps misleading, because the concept of point of view suggests a character's optical point of view, and *optical point of view* seems like such an either/or term. Either the camera is looking through a character's eyes, or it is not. None of these three shots is from Harry's optical point of view. And yet several concepts related to the broader concept of perspectival understanding remain relevant, such as Harry's emotional state, his attitudes, and his position in space. The scene appeals to the sorts of "virtual events" and "embedded narratives" that Marie-Laure Ryan discusses in her theory of tellability. A part of the meaning of the low-angle shot of Dumbledore derives from the fact that it represents what

Harry *would* see if he were to turn around. Understanding the shot involves more than just saying it is a shot of Dumbledore; it also involves recognizing that this view of Dumbledore is simultaneously what Harry could see and what Harry does not see. Framing the question in either/or terms does not do justice to shots like this or to other techniques that appeal to Harry's perspective in complex ways.

For an even stronger example of multiplicity, consider a sequence that seems much more subjective at first glance: the end of the Quidditch scene. After confronting a dementor, Harry tumbles from the sky. Dumbledore saves Harry's life by casting a spell to arrest his fall. With an iris effect, the screen fades to black (figure 5). Another iris introduces an apparent POV shot, representing Harry's optical perspective as he awakens in the hospital to find his friends staring at him (figure 6). If we approach the problem as an either/or question (either the shot is a POV shot, or it is not), then the shot of Harry falling to the ground makes no sense. At first it looks like an objective shot, representing Harry's fall from hundreds of yards away. No—it looks more like a subjective shot, approximating Dumbledore's point of view as he watches Harry fall. But wait—it looks like an objective shot, because the camera is moving upward, even though Dumbledore is standing still. Then again—it looks like a subjective shot because the iris-in represents Harry's loss of consciousness as he falls. The hospital shot seems like a more unambiguous case because the iris-out, the wide-angle lens, and the low angle all suggest that the camera is looking through Harry's eyes, but even this shot is not entirely subjective: the actors are looking just to the right of the camera, and of course the frame remains a frame, a part of the movie's rhetoric but not part of Harry's experience.

Figure 5.   The iris effect represents Harry's blackout, even though this is not a POV shot.

Figure 6.   When Harry wakes up, the camera (nearly) shows his optical perspective.

One way to address the problem is to say that the various shots' status as POV shots remains ambiguous, but the word *ambiguous* does not seem quite right either. *Prisoner of Azkaban* aims to reach a family audience, after all, and I expect that most children have little difficulty making sense of what is happening here: Harry falls, Dumbledore saves him, and Harry wakes up in the hospital. The shots seem ambiguous only if we start with the assumption that every shot either is or is not a POV shot. But there is no reason why a single shot cannot convey multiple ideas at once: ideas about the existential facts of the story-world as well as ideas about how one or more inhabitants perceive and experience that world. Figure 5 simultaneously conveys at least three ideas:

1. Harry is falling very fast. (We can see him fall.)
2. This is what Harry looks like from Dumbledore's perspective. (The camera is close to Dumbledore's position in the stands, and Harry looks awfully far away.)
3. This is what passing out looks like from Harry's perspective. (The iris-in evokes the clouding of vision.)

Pushing the interpretation further, perhaps the camera's movement adds another layer or two of complication:

4. This is what it feels like to be Harry, falling through space. (The camera is not in Harry's position, but its speed echoes the speed of his fall.) Or . . .
5. This is what it feels like to be Dumbledore, acting under pressure. (The camera is not quite in Dumbledore's position, but its speed echoes the rapidity of his spell-casting.)

Rather than classify figure 5 as a POV shot in a yes-or-no manner, it seems more useful to assume that the viewer may make sense of the shot in many ways, both by recognizing what it depicts and by appealing to perspectival logics that take in both Harry's perspective and Dumbledore's perspective at once. Film theorist Daniel Morgan has argued against the longstanding tendency in film studies to insist that the camera's position in space determines identification: "We are not 'at' the viewpoint established by the camera, nor that of a character. Instead, we are able to simultaneously inhabit multiple positions within the world of the film."[11] In this example the camera appears to be just above Dumbledore's head, but the shot as a whole expresses multiple experiences of multiple characters.

The example fuses multiple perspectives into a single shot. Elsewhere Cuarón shifts perspectives within a scene via editing, according Harry priority as the protagonist while cutting to additional angles that give other perspectives their due. A case in point is the first scene in Professor Trelawney's class on reading tea leaves. The scene comprises twenty-eight shots from a variety of angles, mostly cutting between views of Trelawney making dramatic claims about the power of divination and views of students reacting with fear, bewilderment, or skepticism. On one level, the scene's shot progression privileges Harry's perspective above all others. Trelawney asks Ron to look into the debris at the bottom of the cup, and he does so, but the film does not cut to a POV shot from Ron's perspective. Trelawney then looks into the cup herself, but again the film does not cut to a POV shot from her perspective. We still do not know what she is looking at exactly; we just know that she is terrified by what she sees. It is only when Harry looks into the cup that the film cuts to a POV shot, revealing that the tea leaves have formed the dog-like pattern that Trelawney just identified as the Grim. As in the playground scene, camera movement amplifies the POV technique. As a student recites a passage from the textbook explaining that the Grim is an omen of death, the Steadicam-mounted camera pushes in toward Harry. After a cut the camera moves down toward the Grim. Together, these two movements evoke the idea that Harry finds himself pulled toward the Grim—perhaps because the Grim really does have power over him or perhaps because Harry is overly susceptible to premonitions of doom.

The pattern seen here clearly prioritizes Harry's perspective over Ron's and Trelawney's; Harry gets a POV shot, and they do not. Even before Harry looks at the cup, his perspective inflects a shot of Trelawney as the teacher leans in toward Harry to tell him he has the Grim. Actor Emma Thompson, delivering one of the best comedic performances in the series, looks doubly distorted—first by her eyeglasses and then by the wide-angle lens, which allows Thompson to step very close to the camera (figure 7).[12] One could make the technical argument that the image is not a POV shot, as Thompson is not looking into the lens, but the appeal to perspectival logic seems irresistible. Trelawney looks distorted on screen because she looks distorted to Harry, who is clearly discomfited by this strange teacher telling him that he has the mark of doom upon him. Again, the camera's positioning does not determine the meaning by itself. The shot as a whole is expressive, appealing to perspectival understanding via the positioning, the lens, the performance, and other tools.

Figure 7. A tight close-up distorts Professor Trelawney's features.

Figure 8.   Hermione watches Trelawney with skepticism.

Figure 9.   The next angle represents Hermione's optical POV.

This reading of the scene is Harry-centric, but there are
other shots of Trelawney that invoke another perspective:
Hermione's. About thirty seconds into the scene, Hermione
appears for the first time; she is discreetly putting her Time
Turner away. Later, the Steadicam follows Professor Trelawney
to Harry's table, and the camera assumes a position approximating Hermione's position in space. Shots of Ron and
Hermione show Hermione watching Trelawney with skepticism and rolling her eyes (figure 8); the corresponding shots
of Trelawney, with Ron in the foreground, serve as POV

shots, rendering the divination teacher from Hermione's optical perspective (figure 9). To be sure, these shots do not look as distorted as the close-up of Trelawney telling Harry he has the Grim, but they add another layer of perspectival understanding to the scene, nonetheless. Rather than prioritize Harry's perspective above all others, the scene as a whole balances two competing perspectives on Trelawney: Harry's and Hermione's. If Harry's perspective seems warped and overwrought, then Hermione's seems undistorted and detached.

Rather than say that the scene as a whole is filmed from Harry's point of view, we might say that the scene is proposing a basic tension—on the one hand emphasizing Harry's growing belief that the Grim is an ominous threat; on the other hand emphasizing Hermione's more skeptical understanding of the same event. By the end of the film, both perspectives will turn out to be partly wrong and partly correct. Hermione is partly wrong about Trelawney: it turns out she does have special powers, at least some of the time. And Harry is partly wrong about the Grim. He associates the omen of death with the dog that has been following him, a dog that ends up helping him in the end, after it is revealed to be Sirius Black. But both are partly correct: Trelawney's divination act is mostly a fraud, and Harry soon will find himself in mortal danger—not from a dog but from a wolf. The issue is left open, perfectly balanced. From a certain standpoint, any prophecy may be partly true and partly false. Ron has no gift for prophecy, but he tries to bluff his way through class by telling Harry, "You're going to suffer, but you're going to be happy about it."[13] It is obvious nonsense, and yet it is also strangely prophetic—an insightful reading of Harry's character throughout the series.

CLOSED TIME AND OPEN TIME

As in Rowling's novel, the different attitudes toward Trelawney represent different philosophical perspectives about time, contrasting the closed time of prophecy with a more open conception of time whereby actions may alter the future and possibly even the past. Harry interprets the world around him as if it were a closed text, filled with the foreshadowing of doom. Even after the rescue of Sirius, Harry continues to doubt his power to change events. He tells Lupin, "None of it made any difference. Pettigrew escaped."[14] Under a trance, Trelawney had uttered one genuine prophecy—that the servant of Voldemort would rejoin his master. That prediction turned out to be true, perhaps irrevocably so. But Lupin rejects Harry's closed reading of events: "Didn't make any difference? Harry, it made all the difference in the world. You helped uncover the truth to save an innocent man from a terrible fate." By insisting that Harry and Hermione have changed the outcome, Lupin insists on open time. The conversation leaves the matter unresolved, lingering on for subsequent films. Even as he defends open time, Lupin resigns his position, as if the firing were his own inevitable destiny.

The time-travel plot explicitly links issues of time to issues of perspective. As Michael K. Johnson has explained, it is not the events that change when Harry and Hermione travel back in time; it is the perspective.[15] The first iteration of the sequence represents the following events: Hermione punches Draco; the trio witnesses what appears to be the execution of Buckbeak; Harry confronts Sirius Black in the Shrieking Shack; Peter escapes when Lupin becomes a werewolf; a mysterious figure casts a charm against the dementors; and

Hermione tells Harry that Sirius has been captured. The second iteration shows different aspects of the same sequence: Harry and Hermione observe Hermione's punch; they rescue Buckbeak from execution; they wait outside the Whomping Willow to see who enters and exits the Shrieking Shack; they escape from the transmogrified Lupin; Harry casts the charm against the dementors; and Hermione and Harry rescue Sirius.

Significantly, Harry and Hermione go back in time to prevent Buckbeak's death, but the film does not actually show the hippogriff's execution in the first iteration; it only shows the executioner swinging the axe. In the second iteration, the executioner swings the axe again—but we see that he is helping himself to a pumpkin. This detail allows the paradoxical reading that the time-traveling avatars of Harry and Hermione had saved Buckbeak in the first iteration, too. Similarly, several events that seem obscure in the first iteration only make sense when they are repeated in the second: a stone hits Harry's head in Hagrid's hut, and we later learn that Hermione threw it; a wolf-call saves Harry from the werewolf, and we later learn that Hermione howled it; a Patronus charm saves Harry from the dementors, and we later learn that Harry cast it. The fact that the sequence of events does not change would appear to settle the debate in favor of closed time, as the characters appear to be caught in an unchanging loop. However, the shift in perspective paradoxically reinforces the idea that actions matter, because the second iteration gives us a new appreciation for Hermione's agency in contrast to Harry's passivity. Even if the past is a closed loop, such agency allows the future to remain open.

If I am right that *Prisoner of Azkaban* stages a debate between two competing conceptions of time, then it is all the more important that the perspectival camera strategies shift over the course of the film, refusing to remain within the confines of a single character's optical POV. Let us consider the film's handling of the scene in Hagrid's hut in more detail. In the first iteration several shots could be interpreted as *shared* POV shots—that is, as shots depicting what two or more characters see together. For instance, when a shell-shaped stone shatters a jar, Hermione picks it up and looks at it. The proceeding shot of the stone represents her POV—but Ron was looking at the stone, too, so it could represent his POV as well. A moment later Harry looks out the window. The proceeding shot of Dumbledore leading Fudge and the executioner to the hut represents Harry's POV—but it also represents the POV of Hagrid, who has stepped to the window to take a look for himself. When Ron, Hermione, and Harry run through the patch of gargantuan pumpkins, a Steadicam shot arcs around a scarecrow. The rapid camera movement marks the shot as a POV shot, representing the perspective of the students as they race to escape detection. But whose POV is on display? Technically, none of the three students is looking back toward the hut when the cut to the POV shot occurs. When the POV shot cuts to the reaction, only Hermione is looking backward, and then only briefly. Later, all three characters look over the pumpkins toward the hut; the corresponding low-angle view of the hut is best read as a shared POV shot, representing all of their perspectives equally. As the protagonists run up the hill, the camera recedes from the forlorn Buckbeak. The POV could be Ron's (as he is looking back on the cut to Buckbeak) or Harry's (as he is looking back after the cut to Buckbeak), or perhaps it is best to say that it captures the emotional experience of all three, since all three are experiencing the loss of Buckbeak. The end of the sequence shifts decisively toward this more inclusive option. Standing near the bridge, the three characters look down toward the hut (figure 10). The next shot—a high-angle extreme long shot depicting the executioner amid the pumpkins—clearly represents their distant optical perspective on this event, albeit with a slight zoom-in evoking a heightening of attention, but it is impossible to say whose POV is represented (figure 11). The filmmakers have taken advantage of the flexibility of perspectival motivation to emphasize how the trio experiences the tragedy together.

Figure 10.   Ron, Hermione, and Harry look down . . .

Figure 11.   . . . and see the executioner in the pumpkin patch.

Within this shared context, the shot breakdown during the Hagrid sequence subtly favors Hermione's perspective on events. She is the first one to open the door to escape the hut, and the camera cranes past her to frame a view of Dumbledore, Fudge, and the executioner. She is the first to notice something strange is happening in the trees behind the pumpkin patch, and the camera Steadicams past her to frame a view of the apparently empty forest. The reverse shots showing Hermione's reactions do not look like POV shots at this point in the film; later scenes will reveal that they approximate the perspective of Hermione's time-traveling avatar.

The second iteration of this scene handles perspectives rather differently. Ron is not present for the repeated adventure, and the perspective shifts from Hermione to Harry and back again, in the manner of the divination scene. Hiding behind the pumpkins, Hermione wonders why their original iterations are not leaving the shack (figure 12). The corresponding POV shot belongs exclusively to Hermione, as she is the only one who could see this particular view (figure 13). This favoring of Hermione's perspective sets up the twist: she is the one who spots the shell-shaped stone, and she is the one who figures out that they must act decisively in this time-line to produce the results of the previous timeline. Later in the sequence, Harry and Hermione attempt to free Buckbeak, and the film shows several POV shots of Hagrid's hut. Now the POV clearly belongs to Harry; he is closer to the hut, and Hermione eventually exits their shot. The effect is not to elevate Harry but to undercut him. By focusing on Harry's perspective, the film temporarily withholds information about what Hermione is doing, setting up the surprise revelation that she has solved a problem by securing ferrets for Buckbeak to eat. This miniature piece of narrative dynamic echoes the narrative dynamics of the entire film, whereby a focus on Harry's range of knowledge sets up surprise revelations concerning what he systematically overlooks.

Figure 12.   While Harry turns away, Hermione looks and sees . . .

Figure 13.   Hagrid's hut.

Note that perspectival motivation is an optional feature, as is fictional or story-world motivation more generally, especially when it comes to camera movement. The camera always moves for rhetorical reasons, playing its games of revelation and concealment from the beginning of the film to the end. The camera moves for the audience, not for the characters;

there simply is no camera in the fictional world. Perspectival motivation only comes into play when those games of revelation and concealment seem mediated by a character's experiences, as when the temporary adoption of Harry's perspective justifies the exclusion of key facts he overlooks, or when the even-more-fleeting adoption of Hermione's perspective justifies the inclusion of key facts that she alone manages to see. Many scenes make no explicit appeal to Harry's perspective beyond the generalized adherence to the rule that the film should show only what is within Harry's range of awareness. When Harry arrives at Hogwarts, the camera's sweeping movements through the Great Hall shift attention from foreground to background and again to the foreground. Hundreds of (digitally added) candles float above the tables; Mr. Filch and his cat Mrs. Norris are dimly visible on the far left. The camera cranes down to reveal a choir of students singing a Macbeth-themed song. As the camera draws nearer, it becomes clear that some of the students are holding frogs or toads, which burp out the bass notes. As the camera approaches the choir, the singers finish the song and step aside to reveal Dumbledore walking to the podium. This last movement reveals four teachers standing behind the headmaster: McGonagall, Snape, the newly hired Lupin, and the newly promoted Hagrid. The rhetorical goal here is to make dull exposition feel like thrilling discovery, allowing viewers to delight in the profusion of details. Because Harry is in the room, the shot remains within his range of awareness, but there is no attempt to suggest that the flow of disclosures follows Harry's flow of attention, as if he were looking at the candles, and then at the choir, and then at Dumbledore. Only at the end of the scene is there a shift toward perspectival logic, as the camera dollies in toward Harry and up toward Dumbledore to suggest that Harry has locked his attention on the headmaster, who is now speaking directly to Harry even though he appears to be offering advice to the student body as a whole.

This camera movement also illustrates Cuarón's impact on the visual style of the series as a whole. The convocation scene in *Sorcerer's Stone*, directed by Chris Columbus, is much less dynamic, favoring stationary camerawork and small zooms. When David Yates got the chance to direct a similar convocation speech in *Half-Blood Prince*, he followed Cuarón's model closely—with one crucial modification. Again Dumbledore delivers a speech to the entire student body—this time about Tom Riddle. Again Dumbledore phrases his speech so particular passages will have special relevance for particular students. Again the camera dollies toward Dumbledore as he reaches his peroration, and again the camera dollies toward the students who find extra significance in his words. But Yates adds a nice layer of complication to the technique, using the dolly to pick out three separate characters—Harry, Ginny Weasley, and Draco—to evoke the idea that Dumbledore is speaking to all three at once: to Harry, who recognizes that he has a great deal in common with the person whom Dumbledore is discussing; to Ginny, who was manipulated by Tom Riddle in the second film, *Chamber of Secrets*; and to Draco, who is being manipulated by the same Tom Riddle (now Lord Voldemort) in this movie, which is something of a companion piece to that second film. Far from merely copying the stylistic tic of moving the camera continually, Yates has grasped Cuarón's deeper strategy of designing those camera movements to evoke the distinct perspectives of multiple characters with competing interests in the same scene.

THE FIVE SEASONS

On a few occasions *Prisoner of Azkaban* abandons Harry's perspective altogether, showing details that are simply outside his range of awareness. These are some of the most memorable and lyrical shots in the film, not just because they break the pattern but because they do so in a completely systematic way. Whenever the timeline leaps from one season to another, the film shows an image of the Whomping Willow sitting on the edge of the forest. Together, these willow shots form a dynamic motif; call it the Seasons motif.[16] The motif includes the following sequences:

1. Late summer. A six-shot sequence follows a bird as it flies through the bridge. When the bird flies by the Willow, the Willow kills the bird with one quick swipe.
2. Autumn. A three-shot sequence follows a leaf as it falls from the Willow to the ground. Then the Willow shakes off all its remaining leaves (figure 14).
3. Autumn to winter. In a single digitally enhanced shot, the camera follows Harry's owl Hedwig as she flies through the hills and up to the clock tower, where Harry stands in utter solitude.
4. Late winter. A three-shot sequence shows butterflies landing on the grass as the snow melts. The Willow shakes the water off its branches.
5. Spring. A single shot shows another bird approaching the Willow. The Willow swipes again, turning the bird into a little explosion of feathers.

Rather than repeat the same image five times, the five iterations of the motif offer variations on recurring themes. Four
of the five iterations depict the willow in action. Three depict
birds, one depicts a butterfly, and one depicts a leaf falling to
the ground. The first and last show the Willow smacking a
bird away; the second and fourth show the Willow shaking
its branches. The clock tower is visible and audible in the first
sequence, visible in the third, and temporally adjacent to the
fifth (which occurs just after an image of Harry and Hermione
standing in the hospital with the clock in the background).
With the partial exception of the autumn-to-winter shot, these
examples depart from the principle that every depicted event
must be within Harry's range of knowledge. The first sequence
goes so far as to adopt another principle altogether, following
the flight of the blue bird as if it were the protagonist of its
own little tragedy.

Figure 14.   The Whomping Willow loses its leaves.

As a storytelling device, the Seasons motif accomplishes several goals. The late summer sequence does the important job
of establishing the geography of the Hogwarts yards: the clock
tower is next to the courtyard, which is next to the Wooden

Bridge, which is next to the Stone Circle, which is next to the path leading to Hagrid's hut. Having this geography firmly in place facilitates comprehension of the time-travel sequence in the latter part of the film, as Harry and Hermione will retrace their steps through these exact sites. The arc also works to establish the Willow as a looming threat, setting the stage for the big action scene when Harry loses his glasses.

These sequences perform the mundane task of letting viewers know that time is passing, but they do so in a way that comments on time as a larger theme. The changing of the seasons evokes the idea of closed time, as the passage from summer to autumn to winter to spring is inevitable, outside of human control. The clock imagery pairs with the image of the Stone Circle—actually, a gigantic sundial—to reinforce the idea of the inevitability of time, whether it is measured by a machine or by the movements of the sun. In the first sequence sound reinforces the point: the clock tower's gong seems omnipresent, audible from any position on the Hogwarts ground. There is no escaping time.

Or is there? The five sequences listed above recall the various shots of the dementors patrolling the grounds, and the dementors' power to turn everything to ice suggests that even the seasons may be susceptible to some sort of control, after all. Moreover, a key function of the Seasons motif is to amplify the emotional curve of Harry's story arc (as I outlined in the section on the film's screenplay), making his actions seem even more consequential. Late summer happens directly after the fade to black that ends the first act; late winter, after the turning point when Harry announces that he plans to kill Sirius Black; spring, after the time-travel sequence has resolved all of the major storylines. The passage from summer to winter to spring is not an ineluctable process but a rhetorical flourish underlining Harry's goal-driven passage from uncertainty to despair to triumph.

MOVING THROUGH TIME

The transition from autumn to winter is perhaps the most remarkable image of the group. As Hedwig flies from left to right, the color palette shifts from the dull browns of autumn to the cold whites of winter, as if months had passed by in twenty-five fleeting seconds. Fusing two contrary sets of symbols, the image of an owl flying from one season to the next evokes the idea of time travel, but the image of Harry standing motionless in a clock tower symbolizes that he is trapped in time. Similarly, the virtual viewpoint appears to move with extraordinary freedom, flying like a bird from the hills to the tower, but then the movement comes to an abrupt halt, framing Harry trapped in Hogwarts behind the clock's metal and glass. This is the only shot in the Seasons arc to depict Harry, and so it seems to fit more neatly into the film's overall strategy of telling the story via Harry's range of knowledge. And yet the camera's movement is precisely *not* mediated by Harry's perspective. The mobility of the view contrasts with Harry's absolute stasis. Digital magic makes Harry seem powerless.

Of course, Harry does have magical powers, and soon he will find himself traveling through time, led by Hermione. Evoking this sense of magic, the time-travel sequence begins and ends with two variations on this clock tower shot—variations where the virtual viewpoint flies *through* the clock instead of halting on unhappy Harry. In the first, Hermione leads Harry past the clock; the Steadicam operator reportedly had to race to keep up with the actors moving at top speed. When Harry and Hermione turn to the left, there is a seamless switch from the Steadicam to a CG camera; the virtual viewpoint keeps moving forward, magically passing through the gears and through the glass to frame a high-angle shot of Hermione and Harry running through the courtyard below (figure 15).[17] As in the autumn-to-winter shot, time leaps forward without a cut, in this case by eliding the time it takes for Hermione and Harry to run down the stairs of the tower.

Figure 15. The viewpoint magically travels through the glass of the clock.

In the second example Hermione and Harry run into the clock tower, and the virtual viewpoint momentarily detaches itself from the protagonists; it flies up the tower, through the glass, past the gears, and into the hallway, where it picks up the protagonists as they race back to the hospital. These shots do not literally represent anyone's optical perspective, but they do evoke the shared experience of Harry and Hermione. The characters are doing something impossible. So is the virtual viewpoint, which moves so magically through digital space.

THROUGH THE LOOKING-GLASS

Although these effects are certainly spectacular, they are also dramatically appropriate, developing the contrast between closed time and open time by taking the image of a giant clock as a structure of metal and glass that blocks movement and turning it into the image of a clock as a magical device that can be passed through as if it were an open window. In this way the Clock motif connects to another major motif in the film—the Window-Mirror motif. Several times over the course of the film the viewpoint appears to pass through a piece of glass, whether a window or a mirror. The list includes the following shots:

1. At the very beginning of the film, the virtual viewpoint flies through the Warner Bros. logo to reveal the window to Harry's bedroom in the Dursley residence. The viewpoint proceeds to travel right through the window to reveal Harry for the first time.

2. In the delightful scene with the *Monster Book of Monsters*, the viewpoint passes through a window again, revealing that Harry is alone in his room at the Leaky Cauldron.

3. When Lupin teaches students how to defeat a boggart hiding in a cabinet, the camera approaches the cabinet (figure 16). Then, astonishingly, it moves through the mirror on the cabinet door and turns around, revealing the same cabinet standing before the students.

4. At the end of the lesson, the camera repeats its trick, passing through the mirror and entering the seemingly three-dimensional world on the other side.

Two windows, two mirrors. With the help of digital effects, the camera glides through them all. Counting the through-the-clock shots, these six images call to mind several predigital precursors. In *Citizen Kane* (Orson Welles, 1941), the camera introduces Susan's nightclub by flying through a sign and dissolving through a glass skylight. In *The Big Clock* (John Farrow, 1948), the camera enters an office building, travels across a hallway, and sneaks into the interior of a large clock where the protagonist is hiding. The impossibility is the point of these shots, which display the camera's ability to move in ways no human ever could.

Figure 16.   The viewpoint approaches the mirrored cabinet and passes through it.

In *Prisoner of Azkaban* Harry is constantly looking at his own reflection. After the encounter with the dementors on the train, Harry turns to the window and sees his face reflected there. Later Harry sees his reflection in the water as Buckbeak takes him on a flight over the lake. When the Marauder's Map tells Harry that Peter Pettigrew is lurking in the halls of Hogwarts, Harry goes to search for him—and is startled by his own reflection in a hallway mirror. At the series level, mirror imagery extends well beyond this film. Think of the Mirror of Erised that reveals Harry's deepest desires in the first movie, or of the shard from the *Deathly Hallows* films, which enables Harry to maintain a connection with Dumbledore (in fact Albus's brother) even after the headmaster's death. More abstractly, the mirror imagery connects to the recurring dialogue that insists that Harry looks just like his father, albeit with his mother's eyes—dialogue shared by Lupin and Sirius, two potential father figures. When Harry confronts the dementors at the lake, he believes that he sees his father, but he later learns that he was looking at himself the whole time. It is as if he thought he was looking through a window (seeing someone else), when he was actually looking in a mirror (seeing himself).

Harry and Hermione interpret this event differently, based on their competing conceptions of time. Flying on Buckbeak's back, Harry tells Hermione, "You were right, Hermione. It wasn't my dad I saw earlier. It was me. I saw myself conjuring the Patronus before. I knew I could do it this time because . . . well, I'd already done it. Does that make sense?" Harry admits that he was able to alter events, but only because he altered those events in both timelines, as if he was always fated to do so. Hermione's reply is simple: "No!" That reply may seem surprising, given that Hermione had a similar motivation for throwing the shell-shaped stone: she did it because she knew she already had. But in her response Hermione is remaining philosophically consistent. Just as she rejected Trelawney's claims to prophecy, she rejects Harry's implicit claim that he can alter only those events he was fated to alter all along. Given that Harry is the protagonist, it might appear that he has won the argument. However, the previous fifteen minutes have elevated Hermione to the status of coprotagonist, balancing Harry's perspective with hers. The result leaves the question of time open for later films in the series to explore.

CUARÓN'S CAMERAWORK

Many of the film's most celebrated shots—the through-the-clock shots, the through-the-seasons shots—are digitally enhanced, and they look ahead to the spectacular shots Cuarón would design for his next two films, *Children of Men* and *Gravity*. In one astonishing scene from *Children of Men*, the camera performs several 360-degree pans in a moving automobile, right in the middle of a terrifying car chase. In a later scene the handheld camera follows the protagonist Theo (Clive Owen) for several minutes as he winds his way through a refugee camp that has become a battlefield. Although these shots benefit from the digital effect of stitching various takes together, Cuarón challenged his crew to execute the movements in-camera as much as possible. (The automobile had a rig in the ceiling allowing the camera to spin around.)[18] *Gravity* relies much more extensively on visual effects, as in the opening shot, which extends for over twelve minutes without a visible cut as the virtual camera introduces the protagonist and her dilemma. Later the camera approaches Dr. Stone (Sandra Bullock) and morphs through the glass of her helmet; then it turns around to frame a POV shot of the world spinning by before reversing its movements and framing her from the outside again.[19]

In these three films Cuarón explores a concern that has haunted filmmakers for decades. Should the camera move like a person, or should it move with all the freedom that technology allows?[20] In *Prisoner of Azkaban* the camerawork alternates between the modest and the flamboyant, evoking the story's shifts from everyday troubles to outlandish magic. *Children of Men* favors a quasi-documentary style featuring extensive handheld camerawork, the motion echoing the uneasiness of its human subjects. *Gravity* is more spectacular, representing space travel as a kind of magic: the camera can go anywhere, making any sort of movement, from the large-scale (spinning around a space shuttle that is itself circumnavigating the globe) to the small-scale (inching through the glass of Dr. Stone's helmet).

Cuarón's camerawork in *Children of Men* and *Gravity* is exciting to watch because it is so unpredictable. One moment the camera may be inside a car, and then suddenly it has slipped out again. One moment the camera may be watching Dr. Stone spin around in space, and then suddenly it is spinning around with her. However, it is important to note that the unpredictability stems from two distinct sources. The camerawork may be surprising because of what the camera is *doing*: it is spinning, it is descending, it is flying. Or the camerawork may be surprising because of what the camera is *revealing*: it is showing a character who used to be offscreen, it is concealing a story event we would normally expect to see, or it is keeping a crucial detail on the very edge of the frame. Cuarón's best shots involve both doing and revealing. To take one example, consider the six-and-a-half-minute shot following Theo through the battle-scarred refugee camp in *Children of Men*. The film, which sadly grows more relevant every year, represents an ugly shift toward fascism and anti-immigration sentiment in the midst of a global crisis. Whereas other major films about globalization, such as *Babel* (Alejandro González Iñárritu, 2006), show connectedness by cutting freely from country to country, Cuarón's film keeps the perspective confined to Theo's space—not to champion his solitude but to show how his space is indissolubly connected to others, whether he likes it or not. The camera's actual movements in the battle scene are surprising enough: down a corridor, into a bus, and up a stairway, always bumping with handheld intensity. But the real surprises come from the interplay of offscreen and onscreen space. We never know which way the camera will pan or who is going to enter the shot or from where that entrance will come—maybe from offscreen left, maybe from offscreen right, maybe from behind the camera, or maybe from afar. Just as the film exposes the arbitrariness and futility of borders, the camerawork foregrounds the arbitrariness of the frame lines that hew so narrowly to its protagonist's experiences.

Prisoner of Azkaban has a very different set of themes (though arguably it is about immigration in its own way, telling the story of a boy who travels from one world to another and who finds a new community, even as he learns that this new world can be as full of prejudice and suspicion as the world he left behind). The camera is rarely handheld, and on the whole the style is much smoother than that of *Children of Men*. Yet Cuarón's trademark unpredictability enlivens the camerawork throughout, not just because of what the virtual camera is doing (e.g., flying through a clock) but, more importantly, because of what the camera reveals about the story-world: it is just so dense with detail. One of my favorite shots in the film is a simple Steadicam shot following Harry, Hermione, and Ron as they walk across the courtyard. Ron has accused Hermione of allowing her cat to kill Scabbers; Hermione retorts that "Ronald" needs to take better care of his pets. The trio occupies the foreground for most of the shot, but the scene's fascination stems from everything else onscreen: the pendulum swinging in the background, the two students studying on the stairs, the falconer training an owl, the white birds that fly by, the two girls chatting, the sculpture of an eagle devouring a snake, the three robed students with books, the twisted tree, the boy playing a woodwind instrument, the entrance to the Wooden Bridge, and, finally, Crookshanks hopping onto a ledge (figure 17).[21] Harry, ignoring the argument, is enjoying an ordinary day in Hogwarts, and the shot (seemingly so effortless for all the work that went into it) makes Hogwarts seem like a fun place to be. The courtyard is just so full of surprises—everywhere the camera turns, there is a new curiosity to notice. Most of the details are irrelevant to the larger plot, but they make the world seem lived-in.

Figure 17. Harry, Hermione, and Ron walk past a man training an owl.

Daniel Radcliffe, Emma Watson, and Rupert Grint show us what it is like to live in such a world. Radcliffe conveys Harry's abiding curiosity about Hogwarts by smiling at the two girls at the fountain and turning back to get a last glimpse at the courtyard before entering the Wooden Bridge. Although Hermione comments favorably on the weather, she is too distracted by her argument with Ron to enjoy it. Watson performs this tension by adjusting her character's movement, walking half a step ahead of Grint for her first line, stepping farther away and looking away as the confrontation escalates, and then walking backward to face Grint for her final admonishment. Ron is utterly absorbed in the dispute, and Grint enacts his absorption by glaring at Watson, turning pleadingly to Radcliffe, and then glaring at Watson some more as he returns to her side. Together, the three actors create characters who navigate the courtyard with ease, as if trained owls and medieval music were everyday occurrences.

Actors and Authorship

Stories are about change. In movies it is up to actors to show these changes—the sudden conversion, the gradual decline, the hard-won lesson, the surprise unmasking. For all its digital spectacle, *Prisoner of Azkaban* generates much of its emotional appeal via a much older technology: performance. Most immediately, the series offers the chance to see some of Britain's greatest actors at work. The third film introduces Gary Oldman as Sirius Black, Emma Thompson as Sybil Trelawney, David Thewlis as Remus Lupin, and Michael Gambon (replacing the late Richard Harris) as Albus Dumbledore. Even Julie Christie makes an appearance in a small cameo as Madame Rosmerta. These award-winning actors join a cast that already featured Alan Rickman as Severus Snape, Maggie Smith as Professor McGonagall, and Robbie Coltrane as Rubeus Hagrid. Their performances are always vivid, frequently hilarious, and sometimes quite moving. In addition, the Harry Potter series lets us watch a troupe of young actors develop their skills over the course of eight films, mastering roles that grow increasingly complex film by film. For these actors *Prisoner of Azkaban* represented a crucial turning point. Radcliffe, Watson, and Grint had been in their tweens when they started the project, and the series' initial director Chris Columbus would draw performances from them by requesting specific emotional expressions, such as "Eyes wide, terrified."[1] For the third film Cuarón encouraged the stars to take more ownership of their roles. According to Radcliffe, "For the first film, we needed to be told what we should be feeling in these moments. When Alfonso came along, we were all a little bit older, and we had to start making these acting choices."[2]

Before filming began Cuarón signaled the new level of responsibility by giving his three stars homework: he asked them to write backstories for their characters. The request effectively asked the stars to follow the model of Rowling herself, who famously wrote elaborate backstories for all her characters, whether those backstories ended up in the books or not.[3] Radcliffe and Watson wrote about the pre-Hogwarts lives of Harry and Hermione, respectively. Rupert Grint wrote nothing at all, but he explained that Ron Weasley would never have completed such an assignment. Cuarón responded, "Okay, you do understand your character."[4] During rehearsals Cuarón made a point of asking his actors for their opinions: "You have to be clear about what you're going to do as a director, but then you ask the actors, 'What do *you* think you would do? Not you as Emma, but you as Hermione. Okay, show me.'"[5] In so doing he drew more nuanced performances from the actors while laying the groundwork for the rest of the series by preparing the actors for their roles as significant coauthors of the film.

DIRECTORS AND OTHER AUTEURS

Throughout this book I endorse a collaborative-authorship model of filmmaking. This position in itself is not exactly controversial; after all, traditional auteur theory, which credits the director with authorship of a film, has been out of fashion for decades. Still, some readers might wonder if treating actors as coauthors is taking the argument a step too far. Rowling seems like an obvious candidate for authorial status; what do we do with a fourteen-year-old who is reading a script? But *Prisoner of Azkaban* is better appreciated when we take a wide range of contributors into account, from actors to designers to composers. Much of its artistry lies in its intricately realized world, and this world had many creators.

Admittedly, there may be some films where it makes more sense to say that the director is the sole author. Malcolm Turvey has argued that Jacques Tati's *Play Time* (1967) is such a film; perhaps Cuarón's *Roma* is another.[6] (Cuarón wrote, directed, photographed, and coedited the film, which is loosely based on his childhood memories.) On the other side of the artistic spectrum, there may be films that are so incoherent that they lack an author altogether.[7] The collaborative model I have in mind is a subset of a more general multiple-authorship view—that is, the view that in mainstream cinema "there are many authors of a film, plausibly occupying some or all of the main production roles (director, screen writer, actors, cinematographer, composer, etc.), who may or may not be in harmony on the purposes of the production."[8] As Berys Gaut explains this position, a multiply authored film might still benefit from a centralized figure (such as a director) who organizes the work of various departments, but authorship remains multiple because each department contributes artistic qualities—often rigorously patterned artistic qualities—well beyond the reach of a single person. To make his case, Gaut cites actors' contributions in particular: even the most controlling director cannot shape an actor's facial expressions and gestures in the minutest detail.[9] Although some of these expressions and gestures might be incidental, actors deserve to be thought of as coauthors when they use their expressions and gestures artistically—to interpret their characters' arcs and actions.

Gaut's account notes that the relevant contributors "may or may not be in harmony" with each other. Although some projects benefit from harmony, others benefit from tension.[10] Within this framework of the multiple-authorship theory, I would define a collaboratively authored film as one that tends toward harmony, synthesizing the contributions of various artists. The philosophers Sondra Bacharach and Deborah Tollefsen have defended a version of the coauthorship theory for film and other arts; their article carries the wonderful title "*We* Did It."[11] My proposal is that several people who made *Prisoner of Azkaban*—Rowling, Kloves, Cuarón, Radcliffe, Watson, Grint, and many more—could fairly look at each other at the film's premiere and say just that: We did it.

The ideal of collaborative authorship need not imply that each member of the team contributes to every single decision. Clearly, actors make their most meaningful contributions in the area of performance, and cinematographers make their most meaningful contributions in the area of lighting and composition. Big-budget Hollywood movies rely on multiple collaborators precisely because a detailed division of labor is necessary to get everything done. Nor need the idea of collaborative authorship imply that everyone listed in a film's credits is a coauthor (since some film workers, such as accountants or caterers, make no patterned contribution to the artistic form of the work), or that all contributors should be considered as equally central to a film's authorship (since some film workers undoubtedly make more decisive contributions than others).

Some critics may prefer to draw the line tightly around a few central figures, including only those who shape the larger arc of the film (such as the lead actors and the production designer), while excluding those who concentrate on particular tasks (such as the creature hairdresser and the Foley walker); others may prefer a larger circle. As traditional auteur theory points out, a good director is usually at or near the center of the circle because the director is in a position to coordinate the work of several departments: guiding the decisions about camera placement, approving the design of costumes and sets and props, and shaping the actors' performances. However, traditional auteur theory tends to favor directors who go about this job in a very particular way—forcefully. As auteurist Andrew Sarris writes, "The strong director imposes his [*sic*] personality on a film; the weak director allows the personalities of others to run rampant."[12] But a director might take a different approach to the job, cultivating personal contributions without suppressing them, thereby allowing collaborative authorship to flourish. The story about Cuarón asking Emma Watson what Hermione would do suggests that he favored this more inclusive approach while making *Prisoner of Azkaban*. To be sure, even the most open-minded director can still be incredibly demanding. Cuarón's longtime friend Emmanuel Lubezki once explained that the director's success stemmed from his maniacal determination to push his coworkers to do their best: "He never accepts less. He never accepts moments that are almost O.K. There are times on the set when you look at him and think, 'Who is this madman?' "[13] But this mania always serves a purpose, getting the best work out of each contributor. This purpose is fully consistent with the collaborative-authorship model.

THE ARC OF A SERIES

The fact that *Prisoner of Azkaban* is the third film in an eight-film series complicates some of these guiding assumptions about authorship in interesting ways. A skeptic might say that I am still giving Cuarón too much credit by assigning him a central role; after all, he inherited a talented cast and crew who collectively had earned dozens of Oscar nominations over the course of their pre-*Potter* careers. Much of the work took place before Cuarón ever set foot on the set. For instance, at least some of the credit for *Prisoner of Azkaban*'s stellar acting should go to the four casting directors who worked on *Sorcerer's Stone* (Susie Figgis, Janet Hirshenson, Jane Jenkins, and Karen Lindsay-Stewart), even though none of them worked on *Azkaban* itself, which was cast by Jina Jay. As Pamela Robertson Wojcik has argued, casting is very much an interpretive process that deserves to figure into our understanding of authorship.[14] On the other hand, a champion of directorial power could cite the movie as proof that the auteur theory has been correct all along. If, as many people believe, *Prisoner of Azkaban* is more accomplished than Chris Columbus's previous two entries in the series even though the films share several actors, a screenwriter, a production designer, a composer, and other key personnel, then surely the credit should go to the most important new addition: Cuarón. Without disparaging Columbus's skill, it is clear that Cuarón brought an entirely new style and tone to the project. David Yates, who directed the last four films in the series, modeled his visual style on Cuarón's, and his best films aim for a similarly complex tone, as in *Half-Blood Prince*, which manages to do equal justice to the romantic comedy of the love potion plot and to the tragedy of the Dumbledore plot. My goal in insisting on a collaborative authorship model is not to slight Cuarón's achievement but to define that achievement in a very particular way: as the act of drawing meaningful creative contributions from a large team of artists. To give credit to the coauthors, including the actors, is to appreciate the full scope of Cuarón's directorial achievement.

Whereas the seriality of *Harry Potter* complicates the argument about Cuarón's authorship, it strengthens the case that the films' most prominent actors were crucial coauthors of the project, as the actors were responsible for conveying how their characters' arcs changed over the course of a seven-year time span, both before Cuarón took the helm and after he had left the project. On *Prisoner of Azkaban* Daniel Radcliffe had the opportunity to display some of the anger that would become one of Harry's crucial traits in *Order of the Phoenix*, two films later. Rupert Grint's performance remained largely in a comedic mode, but Emma Watson added another layer to her interpretation of Hermione by stressing her newfound willingness to confront her teachers.

Indeed, Watson's performance, as it would develop over the course of the series, provides powerful proof that the actors were not just translating the characters from one medium to another; they were interpreting their roles and modifying them in significant ways. Even before the first film had been released, Rowling's books had inspired considerable debate among feminist critics concerning the strengths and weaknesses of Hermione's role. In an online article from 2000, Christine Schoefer had criticized the way that Hermione ended up serving as a "damsel in distress" in *Sorcerer's Stone*, and she noted that her bookish sincerity seemed less appealing than

Harry's more flamboyant acts of bravery.[15] A few years later Eliza Dresang offered a more positive account of Hermione, but she criticized Rowling's use of gendered language: "Repeatedly Rowling has Hermione 'shriek,' 'squeak,' 'wail,' 'squeal,' and 'whimper,' verbs never applied to the male characters in the book."[16] In the Shrieking Shack scene alone, Hermione whispers, whimpers, gasps, screams, sobs, and shrieks, while Harry roars, spits, fights, and yells.[17] Similarly, Elizabeth Heilman and Trevor Donaldson pointed out that the books often mock Hermione's know-it-all intelligence and social conscience, even as they praise Harry for acts that are simultaneously "brave" and "stupid."[18]

Watson's Hermione comes across very differently in comparison to the Hermione of the first few books, leaving no doubt as to why the smartest student in the school was placed in Gryffindor, a house known for bravery. In the Shrieking Shack, Watson conveys Hermione's justifiable fear with raised eyebrows and rapid breathing, but she also shows Hermione overcoming that fear and confronting the threat. She yells firmly, expressing the character's sense of betrayal by accusing Lupin of violating her trust, and she points her finger directly at Lupin when she makes her accusation. When Lupin slowly advances toward her in a (seemingly) malevolent way, Hermione stands her ground, keeping her gaze locked on the teacher. In sum, these techniques (facial expression, hand gestures, posture) convey multiple facets of the character at once: fear, anger, determination, and the terrible sense that her worries have been right all along. Rowling created the character and the situation, and Kloves modified the scene to give Hermione stronger dialogue, but it was Watson who completed the process of making Hermione such a riveting figure.

ACTING AS REVELATION AND CONCEALMENT

As storytellers, actors represent crucial causes and effects, generate feelings of hope and fear, and remind us at strategic points where the characters have been. In an important book on film performance, Andrew Klevan explains that our disposition toward an unfolding narrative lies, in part, "with appreciating the performer's capacities for revealing *and* withholding aspects of the character's sensibility."[19] Revealing and withholding—this dialectic is the essence of storytelling as I understand it. Klevan's observation seems particularly relevant to the *Harry Potter* films, which derive so much of their narrative interest from secrets and surprises. Perhaps this is why so many established British actors found their parts so enjoyable to play.

One scene featuring David Thewlis and Alan Rickman shows Lupin interrupting Snape, who has caught Harry roaming the hallway at night. As Lupin steps in from the shadows, Snape turns to his colleague and delivers an ironic greeting that refers obliquely to Lupin's lycanthropy: "Well, well, Lupin. Out for a little walk in the moonlight, are we?" Here, Rickman is charged with a difficult task: he must insinuate that Snape knows that Lupin is a werewolf (and that Snape would like the secret to get out without having to reveal it explicitly), but he must intimate this in such a way that Harry's continuing ignorance remains plausible. Rickman accomplishes this complex goal by delivering the line so that certain key words stand out: "Well, well . . . Lllupinnn. Out for a little walk . . . in the moonligh*ttt* . . . are we?" Rickman opens his eyes slightly when he puts the extra stress on the *t* in "moonlight," as if he were sending a private message to Lupin—something along the lines of "You know and I know that I could spill your secret right now." Harry's obliviousness remains understandable because he cannot see Snape's face and because Rickman's verbal emphases are so small—really, just a tiny pause here and a plosive consonant there. Lupin proceeds to put Snape in his place by calling his bluff, refusing to take the threat seriously. David Thewlis keeps his hands in his pockets and angles his head away from Snape to get a better look at Harry. The hands in the pockets, with their untroubled casualness, suggest that Lupin can defeat Snape in this particular battle of wits without trying very hard. When Snape, in a burst of motion, reaches over and snatches the Marauder's Map from Harry's hand, the gesture seems pathetically overwrought, treating Harry as a dangerous threat even though he is just a young boy standing quietly at attention. As usual, Snape's intensity contrasts unfavorably with Lupin's ease (figure 18).

Figure 18.   Alan Rickman emphasizes Snape's intensity; David Thewlis emphasizes Lupin's ease.

When Lupin looks at the map itself, another game of revelation and concealment begins. In the dialogue Lupin denies that the map is worrisome: "I seriously doubt it, Severus. It looks to me as though it's merely a parchment designed to insult anyone who tries to read it. It's—heh, heh—I suspect it's a Zonko product." Again, the line as written seems rather straightforward, but Thewlis's performance hints that Lupin knows more about the map than he is letting on. Specifically, his gaze indicates that Lupin is trying to avoid looking Snape in the eye. He stares squarely at the map for several seconds, takes a quick glance at Snape, and then switches his eyes to Harry. Then he laughs awkwardly and unconvincingly, and his voice rises in volume when he gets to the word "Zonko," as if Lupin were self-conscious about the absurdity of what he is saying. Thewlis delivers the next few lines with more confidence, but the point has been made: Lupin is hiding something. Like Rickman, Thewlis designs his performance to suggest layers of subtext beneath the text.

This scene is about secrets, but the nature of these secrets will vary for different spectators, depending on whether or not they have read the book. Fans will know already that Lupin is none other than Moony, of Moony, Wormtail, Padfoot, and Prongs, who collectively created the map many years ago. He has recognized the map instantly, and he is trying to cover up his emotion of shock. For novice viewers, this point will remain obscure, as the movie provides considerably less backstory about the authorship of the map. Instead, Lupin's apparent prevarications play into the ongoing mystery of whether Harry's favorite teacher is a benevolent father figure or a malevolent ally of Sirius Black. If he is the former, then Lupin is most likely trying to help Harry get the better of Snape. If he is the latter, then he is most likely trying to deprive Harry of a powerful tool of defense. Such uncertainty—Is he lying or not?—extends to almost every single line spoken by Rickman and Thewlis in the film. One of the central mysteries of the entire series concerns the character of Snape, who seems evil, then good, then evil, and then good again, with many moments of ambiguity in between. The character of Lupin is one of the central mysteries of this particular installment, as each iteration of the series introduces a new Defense Against the Dark Arts teacher who may be good or bad or some combination of the two. For these mysteries to work, both actors must create an impression of incompleteness—a sense that they are disclosing just a part of a still-ambiguous character.

Rickman's vocal delivery is so distinctive that Rowling had already begun mimicking the actor's start-and-stop rhythm in her books. *Order of the Phoenix* (the fifth book in the series) came out in 2003, a year before *Prisoner of Azkaban* was released in theaters. In one passage Snape's voice becomes "more quietly waspish" as he speaks to his old nemesis Sirius Black:

"I know you like to feel . . . involved."

"What's that supposed to mean?" said Sirius, letting his chair fall back onto all four legs with a loud bang.

"Merely that I am sure that you must feel—ah—frustrated by the fact that you can do nothing *useful*," Snape laid a delicate stress on the word, "for the Order."[20]

Snape's written voice adopts the traits of Rickman's spoken voice: quietness, unexpected pauses, and a light emphasis on particular words. The movie has circled back into the literature.

Rickman had been voicing Snape like this for years; one key role in *Prisoner of Azkaban* would change much more dramatically, as Michael Gambon took over the role of Albus Dumbledore after Richard Harris died of Hodgkin's disease in 2002. Whereas Harris's old and frail Dumbledore had projected goodness and sincerity, Gambon's more vigorous-seeming Dumbledore comes across with a bit of an edge.[21] It is not that the new Dumbledore seems bad or dangerous; rather, he takes surprising delight in using trickery and deception to serve the side of good. This mischievous streak will seem more ominous in later installments, but it serves several purposes specific to *Prisoner of Azkaban*: maintaining a tone of playfulness, producing humor at the expense of dupes like Cornelius Fudge, and conveying the idea that Dumbledore trusts students enough to know that they will understand his meanings even when he is being obscure. For instance, when Dumbledore gets the idea that Hermione should use the Time Turner to save Sirius and Buckbeak, he delivers a cryptically worded speech:

> You know the laws, Miss Granger. You must not be seen, and you would do well, I feel, to return before this last chime. If not, the consequences are too ghastly to discuss. If you succeed tonight, more than one innocent life may be spared. Three turns should do it, I think. Oh, by the way, when in doubt, I find retracing my steps to be a wise place to begin. Good luck.

For this monologue Gambon uses his body and voice to suggest two conflicting impulses: at first he overdramatizes the speech to ensure that he has Hermione's attention; then he switches to a more casual tone, deliberately undercutting the seriousness of the speech, as if he were so confident in Hermione's abilities that he need not worry about the problem any further. Gambon's Dumbledore accomplishes the overdramatization in several ways: by rapidly swinging his body around from the clock, by lowering his voice to a near-whisper, by leaning toward Hermione slightly and then stepping toward her, and by opening his eyes wide and refusing to blink, maintaining eye contact with his brightest student. Together, these tactics create a powerful impression of urgency, as if Dumbledore were entrusting Hermione with the most valuable secret in the world. But then Gambon shifts tactics in the middle of the line about sparing innocent life. Instead of treating this piece of information as the rousing culmination of his call to action, he turns around to walk away, breaking the eye contact he had worked so hard to establish. Then, looking even more like an absent-minded professor, he stops himself awkwardly, turns back to deliver the line about the "three turns," imitates the turning gesture with his finger, winks once, half-winks again, points, and then turns rapidly to walk away before stopping at the door to say "by the way," as if this crucial addendum were barely worth mentioning. By this point Dumbledore is smiling, neatly contradicting the deadly seriousness of the monologue's first half. In just a few seconds Gambon has conveyed two competing sides to Dumbledore's character: the genius wizard and the funky jokester. Manipulating our hopes and fears, the serious tone signals that the film is nearing its do-or-die finale, even as the playfulness assures us that things will work out all right in the end.

The camera does not stay on Gambon the entire time. Editor Steven Weisberg cuts to Watson and Radcliffe on "I feel" and holds on them until "If you succeed." During this reaction shot, Watson's Hermione stares unblinkingly at Dumbledore, and she holds her arms away from her side, creating a sense of tension and alertness, especially as she leans her head slightly forward. Radcliffe's Harry seems to be totally unaware of the gravity of the situation. In sharp contrast to Hermione's focused stasis, he lets his arms hang loosely at his side, he sways back and forth nervously, and he allows his gaze to wander from Dumbledore to Hermione to Dumbledore and back to Hermione again. The two actors continue this contrasting behavior after Gambon has left the scene. As Ron expresses his bewilderment, Hermione springs into action. Watson delivers her line—"Sorry, Ron, but seeing as you can't walk"—briskly and with a definite ending, rather than letting the words trail off apologetically. She moves rapidly, turning quickly toward Ron and then quickly back toward Harry, and she keeps her eyes locked on the Time Turner, even when she has to slap Harry's hand away. These tactics enhance the contrast with Harry, who seems utterly lost, shrugging his shoulders slightly toward Ron, shifting his gaze back and forth between his two friends, and then staring around cluelessly while time reverses itself. Revealing and concealing simultaneously, Watson and Radcliffe show that Hermione knows more than Harry does, while letting us discover for ourselves what it is that Hermione knows.

CHARACTERS AS PERFORMERS

Film scholar James Naremore writes that our delight in acting derives from a number of sources, but one key pleasure lies in the fact that we are all performers all the time: "Films enable us to recognize and adapt to the fundamentally acted quality of everyday life: they place us safely outside dramatic events, a position from which we can observe people lying, concealing emotions, or staging performances for one another."[22] *Prisoner of Azkaban* is a perfect vehicle for such pleasures, as almost every scene contains an instance of feigning, exaggeration, dissimulation, or self-deception, as when Harry tries and fails to keep his anger under control with Aunt Marge, or when Cornelius Fudge adopts a fake magnanimous persona in his first meeting with Harry, or when Draco pretends that Buckbeak has almost killed him, or when Peter Pettigrew appeals to Ron's sympathy by reminding him that he was the Weasleys' loyal rat for twelve years.

Naremore is particularly interested in the way actors teach us to see that the most ordinary-seeming *social* roles are also constructed through performance. The *Harry Potter* series satirizes school as a place of show, where teachers and students learn to play a variety of scripted roles. In the earliest entries to the series, the satire remains light-hearted, illustrating Rowling's longstanding debt to the optimistic tradition of the public-school novel, where a young protagonist matures as he learns to navigate the rigid social structure of the British boarding school.[23] This satire grows more critical in subsequent volumes. Across the series the books suggest that teachers and students are always acting, whether they are consciously lying or not.

In *Prisoner of Azkaban*, Emma Thompson plays Professor Trelawney, who teaches a divination class even though her gift of prophecy is intermittent at best. Trelawney opens the first day of her course with a speech welcoming the students to class and explaining why the subject is important. Thompson

expertly draws on a battery of theatrical techniques to expose
Trelawney's weakness for overdramatization:

1. Modulation of intonation, shifting from a deep register
   for the initial welcome (conveying performed seriousness) to a higher register for key phrases such as "into
   the future" (conveying performed enthusiasm).
2. Modulation of volume, alternating from quiet to
   loud and back again, creating a rhetorically elaborate
   rhythm suggesting that Trelawney has practiced this
   speech many times.
3. Artificial diction, as when Thompson rolls the letter r
   on the line "reading tea leaves," exposing Trelawney's
   pretension.
4. Overly precise blocking, as Thompson rises from her
   chair and walks several steps to a standing position,
   where she holds her arms out and shakes her fingers,
   like a dancer practicing her jazz hands. (Along the way
   Trelawney bumps into a table, just after discussing
   the gift of Sight.) Later, she swings around rapidly
   and points to a distant corner of the room, providing
   dramatic emphasis for the line "You must look . . .
   beyond!"

The impression is not of an enthusiastic educator winning her
students over with her natural energy but of a novice public
speaker who has been told that hand gestures are a great way
to grab attention (figure 19). Together these techniques create
a vivid impression of a bumbling teacher who overcompen-
sates for her unstable command of the material by resorting to
hammy teaching tricks. The performance is wonderfully funny,

but it is also significant to the series' larger arc. Through her comedic acting, Thompson shapes the ongoing treatment of time as a theme. The more we suspect that the school's divination instructor is a fraud, the more we will doubt whether Harry is right to accept prophecy as truth.

Figure 19.   Emma Thompson plays Professor Trelawney, who is also playing a role.

The students are playing roles, too—not in the sense that they are deliberately deceptive but in the sense that *student* is a social role that can be enacted in multiple ways. In this scene Rupert Grint does a particularly good job conveying the idea that Ron is performing for two different audiences at once: his peers and his teacher. On the one hand, Ron realizes that Trelawney looks ridiculous, and he wants to signal to his peers that he does not take her seriously. On the other hand, he does not want to show outward disrespect for Trelawney, especially since this is his first class with her. When Trelawney tells Ron that his aura is pulsing, he almost breaks out in laughter, but he suppresses the urge and agrees hesitantly that he might be in the beyond. When he improvises a fortune to tell Harry, Ron's matter-of-fact wording ("You're going to suffer, but you're going to be happy about it") contrasts with the hesitant expression on his face, as if he desperately wants to admit he knows it is all nonsense. Trelawney performs unconvincing authority while Ron performs half-hearted curiosity.

Later entries in the series will work further variations on this theme, featuring adults enacting the various roles that teachers might play (e.g., Dolores Umbridge's outwardly polite sadist) and teenagers enacting the various roles that students might play (e.g., Tom Riddle's outwardly deferential manipulator). In so doing, the series will bring another question to the fore: Is Harry's status as a hero authentic or performed or authentic-because-performed? In *Prisoner of Azkaban* Harry's climactic achievement is his rescue of Sirius. With a delightful paradoxicality that is typical of the time-travel genre, he becomes a hero precisely when he learns that he has already played the role before. His heroism is an imitation of a performance he has witnessed; playing the hero makes him a hero. The much darker *Order of the Phoenix* will invert the structure of *Prisoner of Azkaban*: Harry's attempt to rescue Sirius leads to his godfather's death. Experiencing this reversal, Harry examines the choices that led him to this situation: "If he had only opened his mind to the possibility that Voldemort was, as Hermione had said, banking on Harry's *love of playing the hero* . . ."[24] The italics and the ellipses are Rowling's, there to emphasize the idea that Harry sees heroism in terms of prescripted scenarios that he needs only to play out. But Dumbledore will urge Harry to consider another possibility, defining heroism in terms of actions chosen rather than prophecies fulfilled.

Turning from the fictional world to the world of film production, it seems that Dumbledore is right: choices define the role.

The roles of Harry and Hermione and Snape and Trelawney were all prescripted, carefully outlined in book and screenplay form for Radcliffe, Watson, Rickman, and Thompson to play. But the playing makes a difference. The performers' actions—that is, their choices as actors—have imagined each role afresh. As cocreators of these characters—these characters who are so central to the series' enduring appeal—they deserve to be considered essential coauthors of this collaborative work.

Designing a World

Some of Cuarón's most valuable collaborators, such as production designer Stuart Craig and set decorator Stephenie McMillan, had been working on the *Potter* franchise for years. Others, such as cinematographer Michael Seresin and costumer designer Jany Temime, were new additions to the project. Together, this team crafted a world—a complex collection of spaces, characters, and institutions, all with their own geographies, backstories, and histories. Much of the appeal of the *Harry Potter* movies lies in these nuances: the oxblood color of the Gryffindor robes, the echoing grandeur of the Great Hall, or the textured fabric of Dumbledore's hat. The books may describe these features in detail, but the cinematic depiction inevitably goes beyond the written descriptions to specify exact hues, exact proportions, and exact fabrics. Readers may delight—or despair—in the experience of comparing the world of their imaginations with the cinematic world that the filmmakers have produced. Beyond the specific challenges of adapting this particular novel, *Prisoner of Azkaban* represents a larger trend in the twenty-first-century global film industry, where such worldbuilding has become a high-stakes undertaking. If the pull of the wizarding world is sufficiently strong, viewers may even visit a Harry Potter theme park or take the Harry Potter studio tour to immerse themselves in that world more fully.

Although the issues remain distinct, the problem of representing a world overlaps with the problem of telling a story. In the analysis so far, I have defined storytelling in terms of its temporal effects. By manipulating the flow of information, the film generates effects of suspense, surprise, and curiosity. A film's world also unfolds in time, but it may be appealing for many different reasons. A reader or viewer might be interested in the spatial layout of Hogwarts or in the contrast between wizard clothing and Muggle clothing or in the biology of werewolves or in the natural laws that govern broom flight or in the social laws that govern the operations of the Ministry of Magic. The appeals are not necessarily in conflict, since knowing about the biology of werewolves can make the story of *Prisoner of Azkaban* more suspenseful, but they remain distinct. It would be a mistake to subordinate the craft of worldmaking to the craft of storytelling, as if the geography of the wizarding world were only interesting because it served as the setting where Harry's struggle could unfold. The world can be engaging all by itself, whether Harry is in it or not. But it would be an equal error to sever worldmaking from storytelling altogether. Paradoxically, it is precisely by focusing squarely on Harry's story that the film enhances its impression of worldhood; the insistence on the limitations of Harry's perspective magnifies our recognition of how vast that world is. The story moves through the world, creating the impression that what we see is just a part of a much vaster whole.

V. F. Perkins's discussion of worldhood provides a useful way to think about these problems. Perkins states that the concept of story necessarily implies a concept of world: all stories take place within worlds. Arguing that narrative theorists sometimes focus too narrowly on questions of cause and effect, he writes, "Why a cause should be understood as a cause, and why an effect should count as an effect, are matters that can be assessed only within a world."[1] Our shifting understanding of a character's actions always must be informed by our shifting understanding of the context in which those actions have effects, including all those effects we may be unable to predict because our understanding of the world is necessarily partial.

As we have seen, camera techniques enable filmmakers to bring questions of worldhood to the fore. By definition, a frame includes and excludes, showing a piece of a world while leaving much beyond its edges. Settings, costumes, and lighting are also worldbuilding tools; in some sense they are even more relevant because they are a part of the world in a way that the camera is not. They evoke a sense of worldhood because they literally show the richness of the world—the way it is composed of countless details, including all sorts of details that do not necessarily help or hinder the protagonists and their goals. These details evoke a sense of worldhood by suggesting a longer history. As Perkins writes, "The off-screen world is necessarily a world of time as well as one of space. Movies always take us into the middle of things because the film and its story begin, but the world does not."[2] Notice the implication that the film's story must seem like it is a selection from something bigger. To set a story in a world is to acknowledge that it is not the only story that could have been told.

Perkins's approach is so powerful because he does not call for a strict separation between narrative analysis and world analysis. The study of worldhood enriches the study of narrative and vice versa. A more schematic approach might look at a particular design feature—say, the oversized pumpkins in Hagrid's patch—and split the feature's appeals into narrative and non-narrative categories. The pumpkins perform a narrative function by providing Harry and Hermione with a place to hide, but they also perform a non-narrative function because their size, color, and variety give them a great deal of sensory appeal. However, the theory of worldhood identifies another sort of appeal that does not split so easily into this narrative/non-narrative opposition—the evocation of untold stories. How long have the pumpkins been here? Are they for Hagrid, for his animals, or for the students? Is Hagrid proud of these pumpkins? These questions may draw us away from the immediate concerns of Harry and Hermione, but they do not draw us out of the realm of narrative altogether. Quite the contrary: they situate Harry's story within a larger world by suggesting that the world is filled with other stories we will never know.

There is another reason why it is unwise to make a sharp distinction between narrative and non-narrative elements: we can never know which is which while we are watching the movie. As Harry and Hermione wind through the pumpkin patch, every one of these pumpkins *could* become part of the story. They could hide behind this one and get caught, or they could hide behind that one and stay safe. The point remains true even if they hide behind none of them. Every object that we see could become part of Harry's story or part of Hermione's or part of some minor plotline or it could remain an object unused and unnoticed. To see a setting or a costume as part of the world is to see it as charged with potential—the potential to inform a story and the potential to be informed by a story.

This point about the persistent potentiality of narrative applies particularly to works in the Harry Potter franchise, where the background details of one tale may turn out to be crucial components of a later tale. For instance, *Prisoner of Azkaban* introduces a new setting: the Wooden Bridge to Hagrid's hut, which was partially constructed as a portable set and significantly enhanced as a digital effect. The bridge serves minor narrative functions—for instance, by providing a setting for Harry's conversation with Lupin and by marking an intermediate step in the paths that Harry and Hermione must recreate when they travel back in time. Still, much of its appeal is sensory and textural—for example, the intricacy of its Gothic woodwork or the implausible ricketiness of its architectural construction. These sensory details hint at untold stories. How long has this bridge been standing here? Is it as unstable as it looks? Will it ever fall down? In a later film (*Deathly Hallows—Part 2*, based on the seventh and last book in the series), the bridge ends up being very important: it collapses during the battle with Voldemort's army, and Neville nearly dies in the process.[3] In a sense *Prisoner of Azkaban* introduces the bridge as a dangling cause, generating an effect several films later.[4] The franchise does end up telling a story about the bridge—but it remains a single story, always partial, always gesturing toward a longer history no one will ever know. Even if the bridge had never appeared again, its texture would have added to the film's worldhood, precisely by hinting at a history of untold stories.

This is the paradox of the films' design: call it the paradox of incompleteness-through-richness. The design of the *Potter* films is exceptionally dense. Every major character has a unique wand, every classroom has its own layout, every House has its own color schemes, and every Quidditch broom has a specific brand. But the more detailed the film gets, the more it reveals that it is showing only a part of this world, a world filled with histories always incompletely told.

MOVING PICTURES

One particular setting provides commentary on the idea of incompleteness-through-richness. When Harry and his friends ascend the moving staircase to approach the entrance to Gryffindor Tower, they must recite a password to the Fat Lady, a woman (played brilliantly by Dawn French) who inhabits the painting that guards the entrance to the tower. The portrait of the Fat Lady is one of hundreds in the atrium. The subjects of the paintings can move within their paintings; even better, they may look beyond their frames, and some even wander from painting to painting. Early in the film the Fat Lady forces Harry and his friends to listen to her off-key singing. Later, when the Fat Lady is discovered hiding behind a hippopotamus in another painting, she reveals that Sirius Black attacked her with a knife. The paintings that decorate the atrium feature a wide range of artistic styles and periods. One painting in a somber monochromatic palette, reminiscent of the work of Rembrandt, depicts a group of serious-looking men wearing frilled collars as they examine a skeleton; another, evoking the expressive brushwork of Fragonard, shows a woman riding a swing in a forest; another, in the style of Tintoretto, pictures a bearded man standing before a hallway rendered in steep perspective (figure 20). There is a painting of a person's left eye in one part of the room and a painting of a person's right eye in another. Subjects who move from one painting to another look different when they shift locations, reflecting shifts in lighting and composition between each painting. In the second atrium scene, a giraffe wanders through several paintings; it is too large for most of the frames, and it appears in its entirety only when it arrives in the background of the hippopotamus painting, presumably its original home.

Figure 20.   The students approach a wall covered with paintings.

The two scenes centered on these portraits are filled with Easter eggs for fans. When Harry approaches the Fat Lady in the first scene, a painting near the lower right corner of the film frame shows a figure who looks very much like Lord Voldemort. A portrait next to the Fat Lady depicts Cuarón's wife and child.[5] Both scenes show Sir Cadogan the knight hopping through several paintings—playfully, at first, but then defensively. These brief glimpses of the knight provide some small consolation for readers who enjoyed the book's more extended treatment of the same character. A key function of these Easter eggs is to generate fan interest. For instance, the mysterious painting of Voldemort has sparked considerable discussion on the Internet, causing fans to wonder, quite reasonably, why Dumbledore would tolerate a portrait of the Dark Lord on the walls of Hogwarts.[6]

But the paintings are more than just Easter eggs. They reinforce the fictional world's worldhood—its status as a place where no one can know everything. Even if the paintings did not move, they would give Hogwarts a deep sense of history, showing it as a centuries-old place that has amassed a collection of centuries-old paintings. Each painting hints at many stories left untold—the story of the painting's subject, the story of the painting's creator, and the story of how the painting came to hang in the school. Add to that the fact that each painting's subject has a history of interacting with the world outside the frame, and then multiply that by the number of paintings in the atrium, and the result is hundreds of little histories glimpsed, evoked . . . and passed over. The two scenes are fascinating because they feel simultaneously overstuffed and incomplete.

Although the paired atrium scenes develop the central storyline in at least two ways—first, by reminding us of how comfortable Harry is with his friends at Hogwarts; second, by heightening the suspense of the Sirius plot—they serve primarily to situate the central storyline within a larger world. Most of these paintings will play no further role in the series. The *Harry Potter* franchise may spawn many sequels (including the stage play *Harry Potter and the Cursed Child*) and prequels (the *Fantastic Beasts* series) before it runs its course, but I am confident that there will never be a prequel about the Dutch men with a skeleton. The paintings are there not as plants awaiting a payoff but as payoffs in their own right. This is very different from arguing that the paintings are interesting because they hold non-narrative appeal. To be sure, one could admire each painting's color palette and composition as aesthetic traits valuable in their own right. But the paintings are interesting, I suggest, for *narrative* reasons, even if they make no contribution to Harry's goals: the story of the Fat Lady is a narrative, of course, but so is the story of Sir Cadogan and the story of the giraffe and the story of the three girls from another painting who hate the Fat Lady's singing and the story of the man who leaves the Rococo swing painting and enters the painting of the three girls so he can cover their eyes when the Fat Lady tells Dumbledore about Sirius Black. The scene is stuffed with stories; Harry's story is only one of them, and even Harry's story will forever remain incomplete.

SETS, COSTUMES, AND EFFECTS

Even before he started work on the *Harry Potter* series, production designer Stuart Craig had a well-earned reputation as one of the leading figures in the industry. He specialized in period movies and won a trio of Oscars for *Gandhi* (1982), *Dangerous Liaisons* (1988), and *The English Patient* (1996). The *Potter* franchise posed the special problem of creating a fantastic world set in recent years with a sense of history that stretches back centuries. Craig looked to Christ Church in Oxford and Durham Cathedral for inspiration, aiming for something that looked "heavy, enduring, and real."[7] But maybe not *that* enduring—Craig freely modified the architecture of Hogwarts from film to film to suit changing storytelling needs. For *Prisoner of Azkaban* he added the clock tower and its courtyard and moved the Whomping Willow to a new location.[8]

More abstractly, Craig designed the sets to evoke one of the film's key ideas: time. In some cases the time symbolism is quite overt. Think of the huge sundial where Hermione punches Draco, the astronomical devices rotating in circles in the room where Lupin teaches Harry how to conjure a Patronus, or the enormous digitally created pendulum that sways back and forth under the clock tower.[9] (One customer at the Leaky Cauldron is even reading *A Brief History of Time*.) Symbolism aside, these spaces evoke time in other ways: in particular, by giving the sense that each space seems lived in. The astronomical devices look clean and shiny, as if they were cleaned every day. The sundial above Hagrid's hut looks rough and weather-beaten, as if some ancient civilization had built it centuries ago and abandoned it. In the Shrieking Shack, the sense of age comes from the dustiness of the floors and the flimsiness of the walls, which lean to and fro, as if threatening to collapse at any moment. Other spaces create a sense of history by including an accumulation of details. In Professor Trelawney's classroom a huge pile of teacups sits in the corner. How many times has she taught her fraudulent lesson about the tea leaves, for how many students? In Professor Lupin's office a cabinet is crammed full of skulls. What exactly is a Defense Against the Dark Arts teacher supposed to do with all these skulls? The framing does not insist on the skulls. They do not become a salient mystery to be solved. These teaching aids just linger as open questions. The real world does not give us all its answers; neither does the world of Harry Potter.

To return to the language of narrative theory, the sets make sense existentially, not perspectivally. To state the almost obvious, the images depict the Shrieking Shack with gray walls to indicate that the Shrieking Shack has gray walls. This observation is not as obvious as it seems. A movie could depict a room with gray walls to suggest that a character *perceives* them as gray when they are not. Such sets would be motivated perspectivally, not existentially. That is not what happens here. Harry is probably not paying attention to the dust on the floors or the teacups in the classroom or the skulls in the cabinet; some of these objects are clearly behind him. They are a part of the world even when they are not a part of his perceptions. This is another way that the movie departs from the book. Rowling filters her textual descriptions through Harry's consciousness. When Harry enters Trelawney's classroom, he actively looks around the room: "He emerged into the strangest-looking classroom he had ever seen. In fact, it didn't look like a classroom at all."[10] Rowling dedicates a full paragraph to the room's features, including its "huge array of teacups." The implication is that Harry has *noticed* the teacups; otherwise, the description would violate the book's well-established principle of filtering the world through his perceptions. Because Harry is a reliable filter (at least in this scene), the reader learns about the classroom itself and about Harry's perceptions at once.[11]

But the movie goes further, consistently depicting all sorts of details that Harry could not possibly notice. Among countless possible examples, one more set detail is worth mentioning precisely because it is so easy to overlook. After Trelawney has delivered her genuine prophecy about an impending reunion between Voldemort and his disciple, Harry walks by a wall where several names have been carved in wood (figure 21). They are difficult to read. One appears to be Edward Almeida; another, Angelus Moriattis. The latter name, with its evocation of the Angel of Death, lends credence to Trelawney's prophecies of doom by suggesting that the signs pointing to Harry's demise are all around him. And yet the name remains a name, pointing to a person we will never meet and a backstory that will never be revealed. Far from giving us privileged knowledge (such as the knowledge that Harry is stalked by death), the name reminds us of our inevitable ignorance by gesturing toward what we can never know.

Figure 21.   Names are carved into the walls outside Trelawney's classroom.

Costume designer Jany Temime faced a somewhat different problem—not to evoke the hidden histories of long-lost characters but to invest all the visible characters with histories of their own. New to the *Harry Potter* franchise, Temime agreed with Cuarón that the costumes should feel more contemporary to match the shifting tone of Rowling's third installment in the series: "Instead of taking my inspiration from Dickens's *A Christmas Carol*, I took my inspiration from the street."[12] There would be fewer heavy robes and more urban clothing. For the day of Buckbeak's execution (a relived day that will occupy approximately a third of the film's running time), the three protagonists set aside their school uniforms and wear comfortable clothing that expresses who they are as characters (figure 22). Harry, reluctant to stand out any more than he already does, wears unassuming, dull colors: khaki pants, a light blue T-shirt, and a gray zip-up jacket. Hermione, from a loving, middle-class Muggle family, is dressed a bit more smartly in jeans and a pink hoodie. Best of all, Ron wears a T-shirt with his signature color—red—and a homemade hand-me-down sweater that is already two sizes too small, underscoring the fact that money is always tight in the Weasley home.

Figure 22. Harry, Hermione, and Ron wear comfortable clothing when they visit Hagrid.

Figure 23. Each student wears the school uniform differently.

For scenes set on typical school days, Temime encouraged the young actors to make the costumes their own. Temime's directive nodded to the minor acts of rebellion and expressions of individuality that school principals and teachers must regularly police while enforcing a school dress code. In Hagrid's Care of Magical Creatures class, every actor wears the Hogwarts uniform slightly differently (figure 23). Standing in a forest on a hot day, Ron has untucked his shirt, unbuttoned his collar, and allowed his tie to dangle awkwardly. Seamus has done the same, though his tie is curled up into a strange ball. Draco keeps things neat: robe on, collar buttoned, tie in place. Hermione, like Draco, looks precise. (Unlike Draco, she is sensible enough to dress more casually later in the scene, unobtrusively revealing the Time Turner draped around her neck.) Draco's henchman Goyle keeps the robe on but loosens the tie. A Slytherin girl has her robed draped stylishly over her shoulders. Neville keeps his robes on, even though they have been ripped apart by the *Monster Book of Monsters*. Harry, in keeping with his desire not to stand out, splits the difference. With his robe on but his collar unbuttoned, he is not overdressed like Draco, but he is not overly casual like Ron, either. Whereas Craig's settings situate the story within a larger world by evoking a grand history in which Hogwarts has been around for centuries, Temime's costumes accomplish the same goal by opening up hundreds of microhistories, where each character has made specific decisions about what to wear on that day and how to wear it in that particular moment.

Other costume highlights include Dumbledore's flowing silk robes, Trelawney's star necklace, and the very English tweed suit worn by Aunt Marge. Amazingly, the costume department created thirty-eight versions of the tweed suit to adjust to Aunt Marge's inflating body. Cuarón had insisted on photographing the Marge scene with as little CGI as possible, relying instead on makeup, costume, pneumatic devices, and (digitally erased) wires to turn actor Pam Ferris into a floating balloon.[13] By contrast, the dementors were digital effects, produced by Industrial Light and Magic, but even they benefitted from Cuarón's insistence on realism. During preproduction a puppeteer manipulated a dementor figure in the water, and Cuarón liked the way the dementor's robes seemed to move in slow motion. The team at ILM duplicated the effect by adjusting the gravity and wind settings on the software and by digitally creating a faceless creature defined almost entirely by its wardrobe: tendrils of floating fabric that look so worn and torn that the dementors could have been wearing them forever.[14]

Graphic designers Miraphora Mina and Eduardo Lima designed many of the film's props, including the *Monster Book of Monsters*, the Time Turner, the Marauder's Map, and the wanted posters depicting a screaming Sirius Black. The more I look at these designs, the more I appreciate the contributions that Mina and Lima have made to the series as a whole. It is not just that these props look so well-crafted; it is that Mina and Lima have used their designs to express the story's emotions and ideas, the way full-fledged coauthors should. The heavy, furry *Monster Book of Monsters* is just the sort of textbook that Hagrid would assign, and the sleek, miniature Time Turner is just the sort of device that Hermione might wear around her neck. Mina once explained that she emphasized the theme of discovery in several of her designs, which require the characters to work before they can unlock a device's secrets.[15] The Marauder's Map is such an object; to read it Harry must unfold layer upon layer of parchment, each page revealing a dense network of nearly inscrutable text.

For certain props Mina and Lima collaborated with the visual effects department, which was supervised by Tim Burke and Roger Guyett. Their job, in turn, involved close collaboration with five separate effects houses, which together supplied over 750 shots to the film.[16] Cuarón's prior film, *Y Tu Mamá También*, was notably realistic in style and content, and he told his effects team that he did not want anything with a *Terminator* look—nothing too polished, nothing with the eerie smoothness of liquid metal. They responded with work that is very rich in texture: think of Buckbeak's feathers and the Grim's fur or of the digitally enhanced writing on the Marauder's Map, which still looks very much like decades-old ink even though it moves magically across the pages. The effects house Cinesite faced the special challenge of integrating its effects within Cuarón's signature long takes, as in the two-minute scene in the Leaky Cauldron featuring animated wanted posters of Sirius Black. The effects contribute to the film's worldhood: not just because they are seamlessly integrated within the film's space but also because they are seamlessly integrated within the film's complex conception of time. The wanted posters have a history—a short-term history dictated by the wizarding world's culture of sensationalism and suspicion. The Marauder's Map has a long-term history with multiple facets—both the backstory detailed in Rowling's book and the vast and incomplete history suggested by the apparent age of the map itself, which has documented so many walks through so many hallways of Hogwarts over the years.

SOURCE LIGHTING

Veteran cinematographer Michael Seresin had developed a distinctively dark style in his films with Alan Parker, such as *Angel Heart* (1987) and *Angela's Ashes* (1999).[17] That style involves careful attention to source lighting, making it appear that each scene is illuminated by a logical source within the story-world, whether a single candle or sunlight streaming through a window. As Seresin explained, "I'm fairly literal in my interpretation of where light comes from. If I have a strength, it's that I light as naturally as possible."[18] Depending on the layout of the set or location, the resulting images could be very dark indeed, with deep blacks in the shadow areas. Fully aware of Seresin's preference for a single-source look, Cuarón decided that his gritty style would be a perfect fit for *Prisoner of Azkaban*, providing notes of fear and gloom that would complement the more upbeat aspects of the story: "We were trying to add darkness, to balance the darkness present in the book. What is so beautiful about these books is the dance of the darkness—the scary, emotional elements—and humor. That is what we were trying to honor."[19] As usual, fictional motivation serves functional motivation. By using motivated lighting—that is, lighting that seems justifiable according to the logic of the story-world—Seresin would produce a powerful rhetorical effect, creating a mood that complements the director's interpretation of the story.

Note that single-source lighting does not mean that a cinematographer literally illuminates scenes with a single source. It means that the lighting crew organizes several lamps to create the impression that the illumination comes from a single source, especially in scenes where it is logical to assume that only one source is present. When Lupin turns into a werewolf, there is only one logical source of light: the moon. Working on a sound stage, Seresin and his crew used over five hundred lamps to represent a hillside illuminated by the moon's harsh glare.[20] Similarly, when Lupin teaches his Defense

Against the Dark Arts class, it is logical to assume that all of the illumination would be coming from the large windows, and Seresin lights each shot accordingly, favoring backlight when the windows are in the background of the shot and sidelight when the windows are on the side. There are multiple lamps outside each window, but they give the appearance of a single sun shining through the glass.

Such a strategy requires sacrifices: the cinematographer must resist the temptation to add little touches here and there, unless they can be motivated by story-world logic. Each lighting arrangement reflects careful thought about the world of the film. As Seresin explains, "In the world of Harry Potter, there's no electricity."[21] For every set the cinematographer had to decide what the most logical source would be. Candles? Windows? Moonlight? Or sunlight?

Figure 24.   This shot demonstrates the cinematographer's attention to source lighting.

In one shot Neville smiles after he has defeated the boggart (figure 24). A strong key light from offscreen right illuminates his face and mimics the appearance of soft sunlight pouring through a large window. Since there is no electricity in the

room, Seresin minimizes the fill light and lets the shadow areas
go toward black. Without fill light, the positioning of the key
light must be very precise to bring out the shape of Neville's
face; look at the texture in his hair, the curve of his cheek, and
the little reflections accenting his eyes and teeth. Seresin then
lights all of the other characters in a way that keeps consistent with this approach; everyone is keyed from the right with
minimal fill. Seresin attends to the background with equal
care. Notice that the background is bright near the window,
dim on the back wall, and nearly black in the far corner. The
arrangement is logical, but it also satisfies the photographic
demand for separation between the planes, as the bright side
of Neville's head seems lighter than the nearly black part of the
background, while the dark side of Neville's head seems just
a shade darker than the dim part of the background. A final
detail is particularly subtle. Seresin has determined that the
door in the background would catch the light if it were opened
slightly. The resulting highlight increases the separation with
the foreground, adds depth to the composition, and locks the
viewer's attention on the center of the frame.

Even more impressive than Seresin's attention to the nuances of space is his attention to the nuances of time—and
his ability to translate that attention into lighting design. The
time-travel sequence required exceptionally careful planning.
Daniel Radcliffe and Emma Watson performed the transition
scene in front of a bluescreen, allowing the crew to photograph
the components of the scene separately and combine them
in postproduction. The crew photographed the foreground at
twenty-four frames per second and the background at eight
frames per second, to be played in reverse. Over the course of
fifteen seconds, the blue moonlight arcs out of the shot and

disappears, and the warm sunlight enters the shot and arcs into the background (figure 25). For every moment in the sequence, Seresin had to decide where the moonlight would be and where the sunlight would be and then calculate where each light would be in each component of the shot—that is, in the foreground component playing at twenty-four frames per second and in the background component playing backwards at eight frames per second.[22] Making matters even more complicated, the result would be digitally stitched to other shots, producing an elaborate one-minute-long take presaging the stitched long takes of Cuarón's *Children of Men* and *Gravity*.

Figure 25.   The lighting changes as time moves backward.

The time-travel shot is certainly spectacular, but it is also funny: at one point a nurse takes a seemingly healthy man and wraps him in bandages from the top of his head down to the bottom of his torso, like a half mummy. For all its spectacle and humor, the shot still contributes to the central story in several ways. The sun and the moon point forward and back to specific events that the characters must relive: the sun toward the confrontation with Draco at the stone sundial, which is where Harry and Hermione will go next; the moon toward the confrontation with the moonstruck Lupin in the forest, which is where Harry and Hermione must go eventually. Emotionally, the shift from darkness to light reinforces the idea that Hermione's action is the film's third-act twist, introducing previously unknown information that will pull Harry out of the darkest moment and set him back on the path toward a resolution. More generally, the scene reminds us that Harry and Hermione have different attitudes toward time. Hermione treats time as something she can control; she ignores her surroundings and focuses on the tool that will help her accomplish her goal. Harry treats time as something to be passively experienced; he turns away from the Time Turner and looks around aimlessly at the changing illumination around him.

The remaining *Harry Potter* films would employ many different cinematographers, all of whom were Oscar nominees at some point in their careers: Roger Pratt, Slawomir Idziak, Bruno Delbonnel, and Eduardo Serra.[23] The resulting films look different in many ways, but they all preserve the strategies that Seresin executed so well: darkening the palette subtly to suit the darkening tone and grounding the lighting realistically within the admittedly fantastic story-world.

NARRATIVE, DESCRIPTION, AND WORLDHOOD

The distinction between storytelling and worldmaking may be compared with another distinction that is commonly made in narrative theory—between narrative and description. In both cases a distinction that seems sharp at first glance becomes interestingly blurry when one looks at it more closely. For instance, the narrative theorist Seymour Chatman draws a contrast between narrative and description on the grounds that they handle time differently. He writes, "Narrative entails movement through time not only 'externally' (the duration of the presentation of the novel, film, play), but also 'internally' (the duration of the sequence of events that constitute the plot)."[24] By contrast, a descriptive passage may take equally long to read or watch, but the passage describes a state of affairs in which the timeline is effectively frozen. Rather than narrate a sequence of changing events, a description renders "the properties of things—typically, though not necessarily, objects visible to or imaginable by the senses."[25] Chatman makes this distinction in order to complicate it. A narrative may slip into descriptive mode and vice versa. Chatman characterizes the relationship as one of "service," as when a brief passage of description serves the narrative by providing useful exposition in a novel or when a quick story adds interest to a travel book's lengthy descriptions.

The cinema poses special problems for this distinction. On the one hand, the cinema "cannot help describing, though usually it does so only tacitly. Its evocation of details is incessantly rich."[26] On the other hand, the cinema's persistent representation of movement arguably means that it cannot help narrating, either, especially for theorists who consider the representation of perceptible change over time a quintessential narrative activity.[27] Chatman suggests that the same image might be predominantly descriptive or predominantly narrative depending on its context. If a movie shows a bird flying across the sky to characterize the typical traits of a springtime day, then the resulting passage counts as description. If a movie shows a bird flying across the sky because the bird is delivering a crucial message in wartime, then the resulting passage counts as narrative.[28] The difference lies in a trait that I have emphasized throughout this study: openness. When the bird flies across the sky because that is what always happens during the springtime, then time is closed and predictable. When the bird flies across the sky to deliver its life-saving message, it introduces the question of whether it will reach its destination before the battle begins. It might succeed; it might not. Time opens up.

The work of worldmaking—in the cinema, the work of production designers, costume designers, and related craftspeople—is highly descriptive, rendering the details of the story-world with a precision that prose can hardly match. We can see that dedication to description throughout the film—in Michael Seresin's source-lighting ideal or in set decorator Stephenie McMillan's determination to pack Trelawney's classroom with teacups and Lupin's office with skulls. And yet, for all their descriptive richness, these images tell stories, too, because they treat the present image as a moment in an unfolding timeline, with a complicated past and a still-undetermined future.

Sound Design and Music

The din of the Leaky Cauldron, the creak of the Shrieking Shack, the call of Buckbeak: here, as elsewhere, the densely layered sound design in *Prisoner of Azkaban* constructs a world that extends beyond the frame. Descriptively, the soundscape characterizes the spaces and figures of the film's world: its footsteps, its ambiences, its effects. Narratively, the soundscape situates those spaces and figures within an unfolding story-world where events have consequence. During the convocation the reverb of the Great Hall provides ideal acoustics for the performance of "Double Trouble," sung by a chorus of students and toads (or perhaps they are frogs). Later, when the students have been herded into the hall to sleep, a similar reverb effect enhances the impression of the Great Hall's size, making all the students seem small and the visibly packed setting seem oddly empty.

When discussing sound, film scholars traditionally draw two sets of important distinctions—between diegetic and nondiegetic sound and between internal and external sound. The point is not to sort all sounds into separate categories but to suggest how filmmakers can deploy these distinctions in creative ways, including ways that make the distinctions seem strikingly ambiguous. Deborah Thomas offers a good account: "A film's diegesis is the narrative world and all that happens within it—those aspects of a film which, at least in principle, are accessible to the characters—while the non-diegetic is all that falls outside it and is aimed exclusively at the viewer."[1] A key word here is *exclusively*. It is not that diegetic sounds are for the characters to hear and nondiegetic sounds are for the viewer (or auditor) to hear. Both sorts of sounds are aimed at the hearing viewer. It is just that nondiegetic sounds aim at the viewer directly, while diegetic sounds work through the mediation of the story-world.

For instance, when Harry opens the *Monster Book of Monsters* for the first time, the soundtrack combines diegetic sound effects of the book chomping and scuffing against the wooden floor with the rising notes on the nondiegetic score. John Williams supplied the music; the effects can be credited to a large team of people working under the leadership of veteran sound designer Richard Beggs. (The Oscar-winner Beggs had worked with Francis Ford Coppola and Sofia Coppola, and he would go on to design *Children of Men* for Cuarón.) The effects and the score work in tandem to produce a unified aesthetic, making the *Monster Book*'s attack amusing rather than terrifying. One could imagine this scene played for chilling suspense: Will this vicious creature mangle our brave hero? Instead, the scene is played for comedic surprise. At first the book seems harmless enough; suddenly, it mounts an attack. When the book appears to have calmed down, it strikes again. The effects are perfectly judged: menacing and ridiculous in equal measure. The *Monster Book* emits a low-pitched grumble as it sits on the bench, erupts into higher-pitched yelps when it goes on the attack, and honks like a goose when Harry jumps on its back. I particularly like the moment when the *Monster Book* opens its eyes; the lids make a slightly squishy sound. The added sound makes the book (an animatronic device in production) seem truly organic. The nondiegetic score enhances the overall effect of comedic surprise: stingers amplify the jolts, but the jaunty playing provides reassurance that Harry is in no real danger.

To be honest, I have never liked the term *diegesis* very much. The term *story-world* captures the relevant idea in a more intuitive way. The only advantage to *diegesis* is that it can be turned into an adjective (*diegetic*) in a way that *story-world* cannot. More importantly, I believe that the theory of motivation, discussed previously, does a better job of capturing what is at stake in the distinction. Nondiegetic sounds are functional: designed for rhetorical-aesthetic effect, they are means toward ends, such as engaging emotions and interest. Diegetic sounds are functional *and* fictional: they are designed to produce a rhetorical-aesthetic effect just as surely, but they do so by fitting into the logic of the unfolding story-world.[2] The artist committed to multiple motivation faces a dual burden, seeking maximum impact on the spectator without betraying the internal logic of the story-world. Recall that the theory of motivation does not seek to classify textual features into discrete categories; it attempts to explain the mechanisms by which a reader, viewer, or auditor might make sense of an unusual textual feature, under the guidance of the text's patterning.[3] Rather than split textual features into two categories (inside the story-world and outside), the theory proposes that a recipient might make sense of an unusual textual feature by assigning it to the work's rhetorical-aesthetic purpose or by assigning it to the makeup of the story-world (and therefore *also* to the work's rhetorical-aesthetic purpose, which underlies the makeup of that world). Nothing prevents a text from appealing to multiple mechanisms at once. Deborah Thomas's study of the diegetic/nondiegetic distinction is rewarding precisely because she emphasizes the moments that unsettle the distinction.[4] She draws her multivalent examples from Hitchcock and Ophüls films, but *Prisoner of Azkaban* would have worked just as well.

SOUND AND PERSPECTIVE

Whichever term one uses, the category of story-world sound may be split further into external sound and internal sound. External sounds make sense in existential terms: they denote sounds that exist in the physical story-world. Internal sounds make sense in perspectival terms: they denote sounds as they are perceived by characters. When Harry sees Peter Pettigrew's name on the Marauder's Map, the soundtrack replays Professor McGonagall's derisive comments about Peter ("little lump of a boy"). McGonagall is not sitting behind Harry repeating her words; her words echo in Harry's head.

However, the distinction between external and internal is not always absolute. When Harry overheard the conversation in the town of Hogsmeade the first time, he was using the invisibility cloak to eavesdrop on the exchange between McGonagall, Cornelius Fudge, and Madame Rosmerta. Visually, the treatment of the scene is highly subjective: the wide-angle lens, the handheld camerawork, and the digital cloak all represent Harry's optical experience. The sound design is also perspectival. When Harry walks up the stairs, the conversation seems distant and muffled, as if filtered through a door. When Harry opens the door, the conversation becomes louder and crisper. Throughout, Harry's breathing remains distinctly audible: he gasps when he learns the truth about Sirius, and he holds his breath when Cornelius stands nearby. These sounds have an existential source within the scene, but they are represented through the mediation of a character's aural experience. The scene appeals to existential and perspectival logics both. To understand the scene, we must understand that the sound of Harry's breathing is an existential fact, audible to anyone who gets close enough to hear it (otherwise there would be no suspense arising from the chance that Cornelius might hear it and expose him), and we must understand that Harry is the only one who does hear it (otherwise there would be no relief arising from the fact that Cornelius fails to notice it).

Another scene that subtly filters its sound through Harry's perspective is the early scene in the Leaky Cauldron, where Mr. Weasley warns Harry about Black. Over the course of a two-minute-long take, camerawork and sound cooperate to establish the particulars of the space before focusing on Harry's unique experience of it. The initial composition frames a wide shot of the pub with over a dozen characters: Harry, Hermione, Ron, Fred, George, Percy, Tom the innkeeper, the rat Scabbers, the cat Crookshanks, and assorted extras (figure 26). When Mr. Weasley enters the shot, he takes Harry aside to warn him about the threat of Sirius Black, the escaped prisoner who is now silently screaming from the posters on the wall. As they move farther away from the crowd, the composition becomes a two-shot, with assorted extras distant in the background. Finally, the Steadicam steps in for a close-up of Harry as he utters the question that will structure much of the remaining film: "Mr. Weasley, why would I go looking for someone who wants to kill me?" (figure 27). Because the scene is a long take, the familiar strategy of POV editing is unavailable. Instead, the scene emphasizes Harry's subjective experience through sound design. As the scene progresses, the sound seems increasingly subjective, as if filtered through Harry's aural perspective. Harry is not imagining sounds that are not there. Rather, the soundtrack grows increasingly sparse, suggesting that Harry is so focused on Mr. Weasley's words that he has lost his awareness of the world around him.

Figure 26. The beginning of the Leaky Cauldron shot shows a crowd.

Figure 27. The end of the shot focuses on Harry.

At first, the soundtrack matches the densely layered space. Underneath the dialogue, the following sounds are audible:

1. The "walla" of the crowd, suggesting half a dozen indistinct conversations.

2. The footsteps of the characters who walk into the foreground, such as Fred, George, and the Weasley parents.

3. Dishes rattling as a busboy carries an improbably tall tower of plates through the room.

4. Liquid pouring from a magical kettle that hangs above the table.

5. Foley sounds as Fred and George steal Ron's newspaper and sit on wooden chairs.

6. The wheezing laugh of the innkeeper.

7. A diegetic piece of music, possibly emanating from the newspaper, which tells the story of the Weasleys' trip to Egypt.

I may be imagining it, but I think that I hear the crackle from the fireplace as well. As mixed, all of these sounds have reverb, which situates them within the cavernous space of the Leaky Cauldron pub.

When Harry and Mr. Weasley step into a side corridor, the walla becomes the dominant ambient sound for a few moments; then the opening of a door prompts Mr. Weasley to lead Harry to a series of new positions. John Williams's score enters the soundtrack, with deep low strings that establish a mood of suspense. Because the music is mixed rather loudly, fewer sound effects break through. Apart from the walla, the main effects are the footsteps of a few characters passing through the middle ground and the sound of Percy pouring two cups of drink. When Mr. Weasley and Harry arrive at their final position, in the shadows apart from the crowd, the musical score has grown quite loud, and the ambience has grown comparably soft for a room filled with dozens of people. A door opens, but the people who pass through the door produce no audible footsteps. We hear no more chairs moving, no more kettles pouring, no more dishes clattering, and no more music from the newspaper.

Two changes have happened: the score has grown louder, and the room has grown quieter. Each change tells us something about Harry's psychological experience. The suspenseful music sets a mood that evokes Harry's emotional state, but it does so nondiegetically—that is, by bypassing the mediation of the story-world. The fading ambience characterizes Harry's psychological state, and it does so by passing through the mediating layer of the story-world, and specifically through the mediating layer of Harry's attention, riveted on Mr. Weasley's words to the exclusion of all else. There is no one point in time when the soundtrack shifts decisively from external to internal. As the softening of the sound grows more salient, the perspectival interpretation comes to seem more and more plausible. Sound theorist Michel Chion has proposed the term *extension* to account for shifts such as this one. A scene with vast extension takes in the sounds of the surrounding environment, stretching for yards or miles or more. A scene with null extension takes in only the most immediate surroundings, shrinking the sound space down to the experience of a single character.[5] Here, the extension narrows over the course of the scene, mimicking the increasing tightness of the camera angle and the increasing intensity of Harry's concentration.

The end of the scene introduces another sort of sound effect entirely: a train whistle, which provides a sound bridge to the next scene set in King's Cross Station. Fictionally, the whistle is a part of the story-world, though it is temporarily out of synch with the image track. Functionally, the whistle is perfectly in synch with what we see, because it serves as a nonliteral expression of Harry's anxious emotional state. Harry does not hear the whistle as he listens to Mr. Weasley, but it evokes Harry's mounting panic as he realizes that an alleged mass murderer is coming to kill him.

The whistle also sets the stage for one of the most striking pieces of sound design in the film, which occurs a few minutes later. When Lupin defeats the dementor on the train, Harry hears his mother's voice calling out "Harry!" As Harry passes out, the sound of the mother's voice fades into the sound of a train whistle. Meanwhile, the virtual camera moves toward Harry and enters the pupil of his eye, turning the screen black. After Harry wakes up, Hermione and Ron assure him that no one was screaming. Their statement firmly plants the scream in Harry's mind, but the train whistle remains ambiguous. Perhaps the train whistles around the time Lupin casts his spell, and everyone can hear it. Perhaps the train whistles as Harry wakes up, minutes later, and everyone can hear it. Perhaps the train never whistles at all, and Harry alone can hear it as a memory or in his imagination, either when he passes out or when he is out cold or when he wakes up. Internal and external sound are not objective facts about the film. To borrow a phrase from literary theorist Tamar Yacobi, they are interpretive options, and the film carefully leaves them open.[6] By planting the idea of the whistle in our minds prior to the dementors scene, the film opens up the possibility that Harry does not hear his mother's voice; he hears the whistle and misinterprets it as his mother's voice. This reading makes Harry seem a little less reliable, prone to overinterpretation, taking ordinary noises as reminders of his doom-laden fate.

Later, Harry will hear his mother's voice again when he passes out during his lessons with Lupin. In the later instance, it sounds more clearly like a voice, not a train whistle. Perhaps he wasn't misreading the train whistle after all; he really did hear his mother's voice (albeit in his own head), no matter what Hermione and Ron had said. This alternative is consistent with what Lupin has told Harry about the dementors: they force their victims to relive their worst memories.

Returning to the initial train whistle, which provides the sound bridge from the Leaky Cauldron to King's Cross Station, I have refrained from calling it foreshadowing. Foreshadowing implies a closed conception of time, as if Harry's fate were known in advance. But this closed conception of time does not do justice to the dynamic experience of following the narrative as it unfolds. The meaning of the whistle must be interpreted, and the interpretation may change with each new unfolding. At first, the whistle seems ominous, associated with the threat of Sirius Black. Then it seems ordinary, merely there to establish the next location as a train station. Then it seems ominous again, so similar to a mother's scream. Then it seems ordinary again, providing an alternative explanation for Harry's experience of that scream. Rather than settle within specific categories (diegetic/nondiegetic or internal/external), such sounds enliven the storytelling by making it more dynamic, activating different interpretations along the way.

Even more ambiguous than the sound of the train whistle is the sound of the ticking clock that appears during the time-travel sequence. After Hermione activates the Time Turner, there are several audible shifts: the musical score shifts to a quicker beat, the gongs of the clock tower start playing backward, and a light ticking is added to the soundtrack. The ticking continues for several minutes. It is distinctly audible when Hermione and Harry hide from the retreating Draco, and it remains audible until the next turning point, when Hermione realizes that they must save Buckbeak. The ticking returns a few moments later, with a slower beat, when Hermione and Harry hide behind the pumpkins, and it remains audible until Dumbledore and the executioner arrive at Hagrid's hut. Is it simply a rhetorical-aesthetic effect, increasing the suspense by underlining the theme of time? Is it (also) an existential fact about the story-world, representing the ticking of the Time Turner in action? Or is it (also) subjective, representing a sound inside the head of Harry or Hermione or both? The terms diegetic/nondiegetic and external/internal frame the matter as a question of mutually exclusive options, but the film simply does not force us to choose. The pleasure is found in the continual shifting and reframing of what we hear, what we see, what we think, and what we feel.

ON LEITMOTIFS

The great composer John Williams wrote the score for the first three *Harry Potter* films, which featured the melody (known as Hedwig's theme) that would figure prominently in the series' previews for years to come. After the third film Williams left the project, and three other composers finished the franchise. For his three *Potter* scores, Williams received two Academy Award nominations—two of the forty-one he has received in his distinguished career to date.

As several critics have noted both in print and in the form of video essays, one of the most striking things about the score for *Prisoner of Azkaban* is its dissimilarity with its two predecessors. According to Tom Day, Williams had used eight distinct themes in *Sorcerer's Stone*: Hedwig's theme, of course, but also distinct themes for scenes of mischief, for Voldemort, for moments of wonder, and for scenes involving Harry's loved ones, among others.[7] *Chamber of Secrets* introduced three more new themes—including Lockhart's theme, a comedic variation on Hedwig's theme—but for the most part the score reworked themes from the original film.[8] This repetitiveness may be due to the fact that Williams was busy working on two Spielberg films and a *Star Wars* prequel at the time; William Ross received credit for adapting and conducting the score. One might have expected the score to *Prisoner of Azkaban* to be another medley of previously scripted cues, but in fact Williams produced something almost entirely different. Yes, Hedwig's theme plays a few times, and the Mischief theme plays briefly at the end of the film when Harry rides his brand-new Firebolt broom, but the bulk of the score consists of fresh compositions, including "Buckbeak's Flight," "A Window to the Past," and "Double Trouble." (The names appear on the CD release of Williams's score.) For some critics the new material sounds so refreshing that it provides compelling evidence of Cuarón's influence: the franchise's new director must have pushed Williams to make a bolder contribution after the comparative unoriginality of *Chamber of Secrets*.[9] For others the new material is disappointing—not because it is bad music but because it begins a process of fragmentation that will only continue when other composers take charge on subsequent films, compromising the unity of the series as a whole and sacrificing several opportunities to accumulate emotional associations over time.[10]

Williams has always had a gift for writing hummable

melodies. (Just try humming Hedwig's theme right now. You know you can.) He also knows how to compose music in a variety of styles, using an array of instruments. *Prisoner of Azkaban* features an orchestra, a harpsichord, a recorder, Renaissance instruments, a jazz band, a children's choir, and a celesta, among other instruments.[11] For all this variety in color and tone, the results are anything but incoherent, as Williams consistently organizes his music to support larger storytelling goals, most notably in his use of leitmotifs.[12] In a recent book, music theorist Matthew Bribitzer-Stull explains how a leitmotif functions as a "developmental associative theme"; the music builds associations as the movie (or opera or play) progresses, and these associations develop over time.[13] Crucially, the "drama and music develop in tandem."[14] It is not just that the movie plays the same exact piece of music over and over again, whenever a given character or object appears. Rather, the music changes in various ways (perhaps it is slower or in a different key), and it may become linked to different characters or dramatic situations, accumulating rich associations over time. In so doing, an effective leitmotif recalls emotions, and not just things.[15] Bribitzer-Stull credits Williams with reviving leitmotivic music in Hollywood in the 1970s, and he points to the first three *Harry Potter* scores as examples of Williams continuing this tradition.[16]

Some of *Prisoner of Azkaban*'s themes are surprisingly flexible; they shift from one character or situation to another in ways that echo the unpredictable construction of Rowling's nimble plot. One newly composed theme, "A Window to the Past," develops a pattern of association with Harry's parental figures. However, as the following list suggests, the parental figures keep changing, and the music develops to reflect these changes. (The italics indicate some of the shifting associations.)

1. After turning Aunt Marge into a balloon, Harry enters his bedroom and slams the door. The Past theme starts to play, very gently, on the soundtrack. The gentleness recalls the softness of Hedwig's theme, so perhaps it is fitting that the first thing we see in this shot is a picture of *Hedwig* on the wall. The theme begins when the camera moves toward a photograph of Harry's *parents* dancing. Their happiness contrasts with Harry's *sadness*.

2. Harry stands under the clock tower, and the Past theme plays while a massive pendulum swings by and an owl flies through the frame, evoking the idea of *time* and recalling the earlier association with Hedwig. The theme is now orchestrated differently, featuring a simple woodwind instrument that sounds like a Baroque recorder. Meanwhile, the next scene begins in the soundtrack, and soon the film cuts to Harry on the Wooden Bridge with *Lupin*. The music fades out as Harry talks about the encounter with the dementor, but it returns when Lupin tells Harry that he has his *mother*'s eyes.

3. Later, Harry has another conversation with *Lupin*, this time in the forest. The theme begins when Lupin tells Harry that the dementors feed on his *memories* of the past. At that moment, *Hedwig* flies through the frame. By now, the theme is firmly associated with the idea that Lupin has become a father figure to Harry.

4. After Harry successfully defeats the boggart, he tells *Lupin* that he was thinking of his *father* and his *mother* while he conjured the *Patronus* charm. Music plays under the entire conversation, but it only shifts to the Past theme when Harry mentions his parents. The theme retains the association with

Lupin, but this iteration also develops the theme's association with *memory*. Previously, Lupin had been telling Harry about negative memories—how the dementors force their victims to relive their worst experiences. Now, Harry is telling Lupin about a positive memory—a memory he can use to defeat the dementors. The sadness of loss now seems mixed with the bittersweet emotion of (imagined) nostalgia.

5. Outside the Whomping Willow, Harry has an honest conversation with *Sirius*, now known to be innocent. The theme plays as Sirius recalls his *past* as a student at Hogwarts, and it continues as Harry explains that his *father* would not have wanted Sirius to become a killer. The orchestration is more symphonic than it was in all four of the previous iterations. The music briefly shifts to a darker mood as Peter Pettigrew pleads for mercy, but then the Past theme returns when Sirius tells Harry that he would like to resume his role as Harry's *godfather*. Previously, it appeared that Lupin would be Harry's new father figure; now that association attaches to Sirius.

6. In the climactic scene, Harry casts the Patronus charm to defeat the dementors. Harry has spent the entire movie looking for father figures; he has even convinced himself that his father saved him in the first timeline. Now we realize that Harry did it himself; he is his own father figure. We did not hear the Past theme when Harry expelled the dementors the first time, but we do hear it now—in a major mode and backed by an angelic choir.[17] This climactic version of the theme carries with it a dense cluster of associations: the *Patronus*, the *father*, and the idea of *time*.

7. Near the end of the film, Sirius has one last conversation with Harry. The Past theme goes through one more round of transformations, starting with the sound of the recorder as

Sirius tells Harry he has his *mother*'s eyes (musically recalling the scene with Lupin on the Wooden Bridge), then turning quietly symphonic as Sirius assures Harry that the ones he loves are still with him (musically recalling the scene with Sirius outside the Whomping Willow), and then becoming loudly triumphant as Sirius hops onto Buckbeak and flies off toward the moon. In a sense the theme has reverted to the idea of the *father figure*, but with a heightened sense of openness. The adaptability of the theme—shifting from Hedwig to the parents to Lupin to Sirius and eventually to Harry himself—has underscored the point that Harry's search for father figures will continue, even after this film.

I have called this leitmotif the Past theme, but in truth it is a little misleading to give it a single name. For much of the film it evokes sadness for Harry's lost parents, but it also stirs the hope that he might be able to find a connection with them. In the final scene it evokes the triumph of Sirius's rescue, while tinging that triumph with loss, since Harry cannot join him. However repetitive the music may seem when presented in list form, the purpose of Williams's repetition is not to close things down but to open them up. To experience *Prisoner of Azkaban* as a narrative is to experience it as a world where multiple things can happen. If the leitmotif attached itself to Harry's parents and stayed stuck to them forever, then the storytelling would become too static. Instead, the leitmotif generates open questions about what sort of parents Harry needs to find and whether or not searching for a father figure is a good idea in the first place.

To be sure, some of the film's leitmotifs are more predictable, in the manner of the shark theme from *Jaws*. The mood is triumphant whenever Harry rides Buckbeak, and the score is appropriately grand each time. However, even these repetitions may cue us to notice dramatic progressions. The first time Harry rides Buckbeak, he does so alone; the second time he is with Hermione; the third time he is with Hermione and Sirius. Harry may have defeated the dementors on his own, but his growth as a character involves his increasing willingness to help and be helped by others. Similarly, the time-travel theme plays twice, and it sounds very similar both times, albeit not identical, since the clock's bells are playing backward the first time and forward the second. The musical repetition, complete with clock ticking, emphasizes a key repetition in the story-world, as Harry and Hermione return to a previous moment, but the repetition actually heightens our awareness of what has changed: past has become present, sunlight has become moonlight, down has become up, failure has become success.

Another musical theme is so flexible in its placement that it is difficult to give it a name at all, though it seems to be most closely associated with the Marauder's Map. At the end of the Leaky Cauldron scene, a harpsichord taps out some notes just before Harry promises Mr. Weasley that he will not look for Sirius Black. The faint notes are hard to hear, and so they do not yet form a recognizable theme, but the idea of the harpsichord has been linked to Sirius (and, more surreptitiously, to Scabbers, who will appear in close-up a few moments later). When Fred and George bestow the Marauder's Map on Harry, a more distinctive harpsichord theme is heard, mostly involving the repetition of a single note, but ending with a technique known as "chromatic double neighbors," which involves using notes only a half-step removed from each other on the chromatic scale.[18] The twins encourage Harry to use

the map to find secret passageways. The theme plays again
when Hermione and Ron stare at the Shrieking Shack, and
again, a bit faster, when Harry spots Peter Pettigrew's name
and footsteps on the Marauder's Map. Should we associate
the theme with Sirius Black or with the Marauder's Map or
with secret passageways or with the Shrieking Shack or with
Peter Pettigrew, a.k.a. Scabbers? All of the above. The theme
plays again as Harry and Hermione use a secret passageway to
enter the Shrieking Shack, and again, louder than ever, when
Sirius transforms the rat Scabbers into Peter Pettigrew. As one
videographic critic has noted, it is particularly fitting that the
Marauder's Map theme should play in this scene, which brings
together three of the map's authors (Sirius, Lupin, and Peter),
along with Harry, the son of the fourth.[19] We might call previous instances of the theme foreshadowing, but again the term
does not capture the uncertainty an auditor might experience
as the leitmotif unfolds. If anything, the final playing of the
leitmotif functions as a rebuke, reminding us that the pattern
we thought we heard was not the same as the pattern that the
theme eventually formed.

BETWEEN HARRY AND HERMIONE

The composer is also a storyteller, shaping the film's narrative flow by making some outcomes seem likely and others
seem nearly impossible. Consider the use of music in Professor
Trelawney's classroom during the tasseomancy lesson. Previously, I argued that Cuarón's camerawork struck a delicate balance, juxtaposing Harry's optical perspective with
Hermione's, thereby giving equal weight to Harry's credu-
lity and Hermione's skepticism. However, the music tilts the

balance sharply toward Harry. When Trelawney looks into the cup, she reacts with horror to the sight of the Grim. It is at this point that Williams's music enters the scene. Deep and reverberant, with no discernible melody, this music lends credence to Trelawney's fear. As the student Bem reads a description of the Grim from his textbook ("It's an omen . . . of death"), the music builds up and fades away, making room for the utterance of the word "death." The score is not filtered through Harry's perspective; he does not hear it, and so it is not part of his perspective at all. But the score predisposes us to take his emotional and philosophical perspective more seriously. Trelawney may be a comical figure, but the music suggests that Harry is right to heed her warnings.

Of course, it will turn out that Harry is wrong to heed this particular warning. The black dog is no threat to him, and the ominous music proves misleading. But that is why Williams's score is so perfectly suited to *Prisoner of Azkaban*. As we have seen, one of J. K. Rowling's greatest talents is her ability to mislead the reader, generating suspense and surprise by making Sirius seem like a threat when the real danger is an old rat that fits into Ron's pocket. Williams's score tells the story not by making it maximally clear but by amplifying its twists.

Some of Williams's cues seem downright dishonest (in a good way). Perhaps the most misleading leitmotif in the film is the three-note musical motif that connects Sirius Black to the Grim. Like the Marauder's Map theme, this motif employs chromatic double neighbors, and it is first heard in the Leaky Cauldron scene, where it is repeated obsessively on strings.[20] Harry later sees the newspaper headline announcing that Sirius has been sighted nearby. An amplified POV shot moves in toward the photo of Black, showing all of the considerable derangement that Gary Oldman can deliver. As the image of Black gets disturbingly large, the motif plays loudly with brass, providing a bridge to the subsequent scene showing the exterior of Hogwarts flanked by dementors. A few scenes later the motif plays again on a horn during the Quidditch match when Harry sees the storm clouds take the shape of the Grim. Much later, the motif plays (again in brass, backed by bells) when Harry sees Sirius in the Shrieking Shack, at the precise moment when it looks like Trelawney's prophecy of doom will come true. The three-note motif is so memorable that it builds an instant connection, linking Sirius Black to the Grim. But the connection was always illusory: the black dog is Sirius and not a harbinger of death. Harry sees the Grim in the clouds not because Trelawney's prophecy was true but because he is prone to see omens where they do not exist.

Harry and Hermione cannot hear the harpsichord or the strings or any of the other leitmotifs discussed above. The music is rhetorical and aesthetic, played for the listener's benefit alone. As such, these musical cues remain outside the logic of perspectival motivation, unshaped by any character filter. Nevertheless, they function in relation to cinematic point of view, precisely by shaping the listener's knowledge of and attitude toward upcoming events. At the risk of sounding too neat, I will put it this way: the music puts listener-viewers in an epistemic position somewhere between Harry and Hermione. Not geographically between them, of course; they are in their world, and we are in ours. But when it comes to certain crucial story-world events, we often know a little bit more than Harry and a little less than Hermione. Following Rowling, Kloves has structured the story so that Harry is in nearly every scene, but Harry is a surprisingly oblivious protagonist. Think of all the things he does not know. He does not know that Sirius is innocent, that the rat is Peter, that Peter is the guilty party, that Sirius is an Animagus, that Lupin is a werewolf, that Hermione can travel in time, or even that his future-self saved his past-self from the dementors. (Nor does he know that Snape is more benevolent than he seems or that Dumbledore is more complicated, but these are revelations for later installments of the tale.) While Hermione is also surprised by some of these revelations, she manages to guess a few of them ahead of time: she knows all about the time travel, of course; she claims to have known about Lupin's identity for months; and she manages to guess the truth about Harry's future-self a few moments before he does. The film challenges its listener-viewers to guess these revelations, too, and it consistently provides them with the clues they need to do so, without making it so easy as to rob the experience of surprise. Music is a major source of these clues, even if some of the clues turn out to be unreliable. The thrilling nature of the Buckbeak theme makes it easy to guess that Buckbeak will play a positive role in the film's climax, but the ominous nature of the Sirius Black–Grim theme makes it comparatively hard to predict that Black wishes Harry well and that the Grim is a false sign.

In a curious way, Williams's music does for the listener what Rowling's prose does for the reader. So many of Rowling's character names involve clever wordplay, often drawing on the author's training in Classics: Remus Lupin, Minerva McGonagall, Severus Snape, Sybil Trelawney.[21] These names function as clues, encouraging readers to guess at future developments. Sometimes the clues are reliable. Minerva McGonagall is indeed as wise as her namesake goddess, and

Remus Lupin is quite literally wolf-like. But some of the clues are deeply unreliable. The name Sirius Black evokes the image of a black dog (because *Sirius* refers to the Dog Star) and the idea of grimness (because the homophone *serious* is a synonym for the adjective *grim*). Such wordplay aims to trick readers into thinking that Sirius is a mortal threat to Harry, but he is not. From the standpoint of the diegetic/nondiegetic distinction, the names have a curious status. Technically, each name is a part of the story-world, but the wordplay exists on the rhetorical-aesthetic dimension. Hermione figures out that Lupin is a werewolf, but not because she has interpreted the symbolism in his name. That symbolism is for the reader alone. With the help of the wordplay, a savvy reader can stay one step ahead of Harry, even as Hermione manages to stay several steps ahead of everyone but Dumbledore. Williams's music unfolds in that same rhetorical-aesthetic dimension. It bypasses the story-world and aims at listener-viewers directly, letting them guess a few plot twists before they happen without giving them the specific insights of a Hermione, much less the near-omniscient knowledge of a Dumbledore.

As Deborah Thomas has explained, a film's cinematic point of view is not reducible to the camera's positioning; it "includes an attitude or orientation toward the various characters."[22] Sound effects and ambience work through the mediation of the story-world, and the score typically does not, but both manipulate the viewers' overall orientation toward that world. Beggs's team of sound experts has given the world density and richness; Williams's score has emphasized connections and progressions. Together, they have contributed to the film's point of view.

Conclusion

My account of the film's collaborative authorship is not the only story to be told about the production. The film is surrounded by numerous paratexts—interviews, DVD supplements, even a theme park—and each paratext provides an interpretation of the film's authorship.[1] For instance, the Blu-Ray boxed set of all eight *Harry Potter* films includes several featurettes presenting interviews with all the key contributors. The contributors tell at least four kinds of stories, each resting on different assumptions about authorship. In one sort of authorship story, Rowling is celebrated as the primary author of the series; the job of the film crew is defined as the work of translation. Producer Mark Radcliffe offers a version of this account when he says, "Jo created this world. We wanted to stay true to it and organic to it. And that's been our mission."[2] A second version emphasizes transformation over translation, acknowledging Rowling as the primary author while insisting that the filmmakers had to make changes to stay true to the books. Steve Kloves takes this position: "Jo wants the movies to be faithful to the books. On the other hand, she realizes that they're completely different mediums." A third story veers toward traditional auteurism by crediting Cuarón with making a vital contribution to the series. Producer David Heyman says, "When [Rowling] met Alfonso, he talked about his vision for the film. . . . I think it's very, very important that

Alfonso Cuarón be allowed to make this his own film." This
need not imply that Cuarón has completely remade the work;
indeed, Rowling herself champions Cuarón's contributions and
adds that "in this case the book and the director were really
made for each other." A fourth story emphasizes the depth and
breadth of the collaboration. Discussing the brilliant design
of the Shrieking Shack set (which sways back and forth on a
movable rig), Cuarón tries to give credit to Stuart Craig, who
tries to give credit back to Cuarón. The other featurettes in
the boxed set go even further in this collaborative direction,
offering a behind-the-scenes look at the involvement of various contributors, such as Amanda Knight, the chief makeup
designer, and Gary Gero, the animal supervisor.[3]

Another crucial paratext—the Warner Bros. Studio Tour
in Leavesden, England—offers its own variations on all four
stories, but above all it serves as a monument to collaborative
authorship. While giving due credit to Rowling and the four
feature-film directors, the tour's main achievement is to reveal
how much work went into every detail appearing onscreen:
how a portion of the Wooden Bridge was transported to
Scotland for location filming, how an animatronic Buckbeak
was built even though the version onscreen is almost entirely
digital, how the paintings in the stairwell were based on portraits of various crew members and their families.

There are commercial justifications for all four of these
tales of authorship. The argument that everyone worked to
realize Rowling's vision appeals to the most dedicated fans of
the books, who will be more likely to support the films if they
carry the author's imprimatur. The argument that the film is
the same-but-different assures readers that they will be paying
for something new. The argument that Cuarón put his special

stamp on the film extends the appeal to cinephiles, who might be more likely to see a children's film if they can be assured that a great director has managed to make it dark and strange. And the argument that the film had multiple authors working in collaboration serves many marketing goals, not the least of which is getting countless tourists to travel to Leavesden to see a studio tour that puts collaborative authorship on such spectacular display. A skeptic might say that my endorsement of the collaborative authorship model is merely proof that I was one of those tourists.

In answer to the skeptic, I will close my analysis with a very different piece of evidence that collaborative authorship provides a useful framework for understanding this particular film. The collaborative authorship takes on added significance when we recognize that the movie is *about* collaboration on the level of its story-world. For much of the film Harry is stuck at Hogwarts, isolated from his friends. He sits alone in the clock tower and mopes, or he stays up late at night staring at the Marauder's Map, tracking the movements of friends and enemies without truly interacting. He has a few moments of joy, such as the flight on Buckbeak's back, but these, too, can be surprisingly solitary. Alone, Harry is passive and goalless. When he finally joins forces with Hermione in the time-travel sequence, the shift toward collaboration makes Harry more active, not less. Similarly, Hermione has spent much of the film using the Time Turner to further her own scholarly ambitions. When she throws the Time Turner over Harry's shoulders, her collaborative action turns her into an active co-protagonist of the film. This tale of magical collaboration is not exactly a metaphor for filmmaking, but there is a genuine affinity between the theme of the movie and the ethos of the craft that produced it—an ethos insisting that multiple authors are better than one.

The film represents this shift toward mutually beneficial collaboration by deploying a significant shift in narrational tactics. For much of the film the perspective has been focalized through Harry, revealing events as Harry experiences them. In the time-travel sequence the point of view expands to include Hermione's perspective, as well. At no time is the cinematic point of view reducible to any one character's perspective. That is not how cinematic point of view works. The film's point of view establishes an orientation toward the characters, and in *Prisoner of Azkaban* that orientation mixes sympathy with skepticism: sympathy for Harry's plight, along with the skeptical awareness that his limited perspective routinely leads him to make mistakes. Indeed, the skepticism bolsters the sympathy, for the film's restricted range leads viewers to make some of the same mistakes that Harry makes. In his groundbreaking essay on worldhood, V. F. Perkins writes, "Since the film's characters are in a world, their knowledge of it must be partial, and their perception of it may be, in almost any respect, distorted or deluded." This is already a wise observation, but Perkins

Figure 28.   Harry, Hermione, and the clock.

goes further: "But that applies to us, too, as observers of their world and their understandings."[4] When Harry, our filtering perspective, is deluded, we are too. The film's restricted storytelling strategy is a setup for misdirection and surprise, forcing us to experience his closed, passive, and mistaken view of time before expanding to include Hermione's more open, active, and knowing view.

The film comes to an end with a scene showing Harry riding the new broom gifted to him by Sirius. The closing freeze-frame is perhaps the weakest image in the entire film, shifting attention back toward Harry after the film has achieved such a remarkable balance of Harry's and Hermione's perspectives. I prefer to think of a shot in the hospital scene, just after the time-travel triumph, as the true closing image of the film: Hermione on one side, Harry on the other, with blue moonlight illuminating the clock in the background (figure 28). The image sums up everything we have seen while preparing us for future installments in the franchise. As a franchise film, as a work of digital cinema, as a work of collaborative authorship, and above all as a thoroughly engaging demonstration of the art of storytelling, *Harry Potter and the Prisoner of Azkaban* is an essential work of twenty-first century cinema.

Acknowledgments

Several years ago I added *Harry Potter and the Prisoner of Azkaban* to my Intro to Film syllabus—a decision I have never regretted. I want to thank my students at Trinity University for helping me to appreciate the film's many layers. A few years later Donna Kornhaber invited me to contribute a volume to this exciting new series. Donna provided encouragement throughout the process, and her comments on the manuscript were always on-point. Thanks also to Jim Burr at the University of Texas Press, both for his support and for being so open to the idea that a *Harry Potter* movie might be a worthy addition to the list of 21st Century Film Essentials. Leslie Tingle provided expert copyediting, and editor Lynne Ferguson guided the manuscript through the production process with efficiency and care. John Alberti, James Walters, and Dana Polan read the complete manuscript and offered excellent feedback and advice from multiple perspectives. I greatly appreciate all their insights. In October 2019 I traveled to the United Kingdom, where Catherine Grant, John Gibbs, and Helen Hanson allowed me to present my ideas about *Harry Potter* to audiences at Birkbeck, University of London; the University of Reading; and the University of Exeter, respectively. Thanks to all three for making me feel welcome and to the audiences at those talks for their thoughtful questions and comments. A Public Humanities Fellowship, granted by Trinity University's

Humanities Collective, helped to cover the costs of the trip. The Collective's Rubén Dupertuis and Tim O'Sullivan generously embraced the project and its accompanying video essay as a work of humanities scholarship. Conversations with Kimberlyn Montford, Julie Post, and Andrew Kania helped deepen my thinking about the film's score. Finally, I thank Lisa Jasinski, who has sustained this project in so many ways—by enjoying all eight *Harry Potter* movies with me, by accompanying me to England for the Warner Bros. Studio Tour, and by adding a touch of Slytherin wit to my Hufflepuff prose.

Notes

INTRODUCTION

1. Cuarón, quoted in Bob McCabe, *Harry Potter Page to Screen: The Complete Filmmaking Journey*, updated ed. (New York: Harper Design, 2018), 93.
2. Although serial storytelling surged in the twenty-first century, it has a longer history in the cinema and beyond. For a useful overview, see Frank Krutnik and Kathleen Loock, "Exploring Film Seriality: An Introduction," *Film Studies* 17, no. 1 (2018): 1–15.
3. Kristin Thompson, *The Frodo Franchise:* The Lord of the Rings *and Modern Hollywood* (Berkeley: University of California Press, 2007), 9.
4. Box Office Mojo lists the film's worldwide gross at just over $795 million. This figure does not include other revenue sources, such as DVD sales and screenings on cable television. See "Harry Potter and the Prisoner of Azkaban," Box Office Mojo, https://www.boxofficemojo.com/release/rl1449887233/.
5. For a defense of the idea that mainstream films in general have multiple authors, see Berys Gaut, *A Philosophy of Cinematic Art* (New York: Cambridge University Press, 2010), 98–151. For a useful summary of these debates, see Katherine Thomson-Jones, "Authorship," in *Aesthetics and Film* (New York: Continuum, 2008), 40–56.
6. The classic account of focalization is in Gérard Genette, *Narrative Discourse: An Essay in Method*, trans. Jane E. Lewin (Ithaca, NY: Cornell University Press, 1980), 189–194. Seymour Chatman introduces the term *filter* as an alternative

in *Coming to Terms: The Rhetoric of Narrative in Fiction and Film* (Ithaca, NY: Cornell University Press, 1990), 143.

7. On the relation between gaps and the narrative effects of suspense, curiosity, and surprise, see Meir Sternberg, "Narrativity: From Objectivist to Functional Paradigm," *Poetics Today* 31, no. 3 (Fall 2010): 640–641.

8. Cuarón, quoted in McCabe, *Harry Potter Page to Screen*, 97.

9. V. F. Perkins, "Where Is the World? The Horizon of Events in Movie Fiction," in *Style and Meaning: Studies in the Detailed Analysis of Film*, ed. John Gibbs and Douglas Pye (Manchester: Manchester University Press, 2005), 20.

10. Deborah Thomas, *Beyond Genre: Melodrama, Comedy, and Romance in Hollywood Film* (Moffat, UK: Cameron and Hollis, 2000), 20.

11. George M. Wilson, *Narration in Light: Studies in Cinematic Point of View* (Baltimore, MD: Johns Hopkins University Press, 1986).

12. On the difference between perspectival and existential motivation and their joint status as mimetic motivations, see Meir Sternberg, "Mimesis and Motivation: The Two Faces of Fictional Coherence," *Poetics Today* 33, no. 3–4 (Fall–Winter 2012): 453–457.

13. Gary Saul Morson, "Narrativeness," *New Literary History* 34, no. 1 (Winter 2003): 62.

POINT OF VIEW IN THE NOVELS

1. Rowling is the screenwriter of the first two *Fantastic Beasts* movies. She is also a producer of that franchise as well as the last two *Harry Potter* films.

2. Harold Bloom, "Can 35 Million Book Buyers Be Wrong? Yes," *Wall Street Journal*, July 11, 2000.

3. For a powerful account of Rowling's handling of several literary sources, see Beatrice Groves, *Literary Allusion in Harry Potter* (New York: Routledge, 2017).

4. Genette, *Narrative Discourse*, 186.

5. Chatman, *Coming to Terms*, 143, 144.

6. Chatman, *Coming to Terms*, 149.

7. J. K. Rowling, "From Mr. Darcy to Harry Potter by Way of Lolita," *Sunday Herald*, 21 May 2000, http://www.accio -quote.org/articles/2000/0500-heraldsun-rowling.html. For more on Austen's influence, see John Granger, *Unlocking Harry Potter: Five Keys for the Serious Reader* (Wayne, PA: Zossima Press, 2007), 34–38; and Groves, *Literary Allusion in Harry Potter*, 98–120. Both books have guided me to several online sources documenting Rowling's opinions.

8. J. K. Rowling, *Harry Potter and the Sorcerer's Stone* (New York: Scholastic, 1997), 2.

9. J. K. Rowling, *Harry Potter and the Chamber of Secrets* (New York: Scholastic, 1998), 303–304.

10. J. K. Rowling, *Harry Potter and the Goblet of Fire* (New York: Scholastic, 2000), 351.

11. J. K. Rowling, *Harry Potter and the Prisoner of Azkaban* (New York: Scholastic, 1999), 172.

12. J. K. Rowling, *Harry Potter and the Order of the Phoenix* (New York: Scholastic, 2003), 548. See also the passage in *Deathly Hallows* where Harry wishes he knew Legilimency so he could read Hermione's mind. J. K. Rowling, *Harry Potter and the Deathly Hallows* (New York: Scholastic, 2007), 128.

13. Rowling, *Prisoner of Azkaban*, 213.

14. Rowling, *Order of the Phoenix*, 166–167.

15. J. K. Rowling, *Harry Potter and the Half-Blood Prince* (New York: Scholastic, 2005), 292.

16. On the difference between range and depth, see David Bordwell, *Narration in the Fiction Film* (Madison: University of Wisconsin Press, 1985), 58.

17. Rowling, *Order of the Phoenix*, 127.

18. Rowling, *Order of the Phoenix*, 156.

19. Rowling, *Chamber of Secrets*, 106.

20. Rowling, *Goblet of Fire*, 216.

21. Genette, *Narrative Discourse*, 67. For another useful discussion of prolepses, see Jonas Grethlein, "The Narrative Configuration of Time beyond Ricœur," *Poetics Today* 31, no. 2 (Summer 2010): 319–327.

22. Rowling, *Goblet of Fire*, 192.

23. For a similar argument, see Jørgen Riber Christensen and Thessa Jensen, "Magical and Mundane Narrative Devices," in *Transmedia Harry Potter: Essays on Storytelling across Platforms*, ed. Christopher Bell (Jefferson, NC: McFarland & Co., 2019), 146.

24. Rowling has insisted that the Pensieve reflects reality rather than memory. It allows the subject to discover details of the preserved event that the original experiencer did not notice at the time. See Melissa Anelli and Emerson Spartz, "The Leaky Cauldron and Mugglenet Interview Joanne Kathleen Rowling: Part Three," Leaky Cauldron, 16 July 2005, http://www.accio -quote.org/articles/2005/0705-tlc_mugglenet-anelli-3.htm.

25. Rowling, *Deathly Hallows*, 134.

26. Sternberg, "Narrativity," 637. I quote and discuss this passage in Patrick Keating, *The Dynamic Frame: Camera Movement in Classical Hollywood* (New York: Columbia University Press, 2019), 91, 243.

27. Sternberg, "Narrativity," 640–641.

28. On the series' gradually darkening tone, see Amanda Cockrell, "Harry Potter and the Secret Password: Finding Our Way in the Magical Genre," in *The Ivory Tower and Harry Potter*, ed. Lana A. Whited (Columbia: University of Missouri Press, 2002), 25–26.

29. For another analysis of Rowling's writing in terms of unanswered questions, see Anna Gunder, "The Migration of Media: Harry Potter in Print and Pixels," in *Critical Perspectives on Harry Potter*, 2nd ed., ed. Elizabeth E. Heilman (New York: Routledge, 2009), 301.

30. According to Rowling, "Lupin's condition of lycanthropy (being a werewolf) was a metaphor for those illnesses that carry a stigma, like HIV and AIDS." J. K. Rowling, "Remus Lupin," *Wizarding World*, 10 August 2015, https://www .wizardingworld.com/writing-by-jk-rowling/remus-lupin.

31. Eliza T. Dresang, "Hermione Granger and the Heritage of Gender," in Whited, *Ivory Tower and Harry Potter*, 230.

32. Dumbledore's exact words are: "You are setting too much store by the prophecy!" Rowling, *Half-Blood Prince*, 509.

33. For a detailed discussion of the theme of destiny in the series, see Lisa Hopkins, "Harry Potter and Narratives of Destiny," in *Reading Harry Potter Again: New Critical Essays*, ed. Giselle Liza Anatol (Santa Barbara: Praeger, 2009), 63–75.

34. Gary Saul Morson, *Narrative and Freedom: The Shadows of Time* (New Haven, CT: Yale University Press, 1994), 42. Rowling specifically cites Shakespeare's Macbeth as an influence: "If Macbeth hadn't met the witches, would he have killed Duncan? Would any of it have happened? Is it fated or did he make it happen? I believe he made it happen." Rowling, quoted in Anelli and Spartz, "The Leaky Cauldron and Mugglenet."

35. This account of suspense draws on Noël Carroll, "Toward a Theory of Film Suspense," in *Theorizing the Moving Image* (New York: Cambridge University Press, 1996), 94–117.

36. For a statement of the problem and a resolution, see Noël Carroll, "The Paradox of Suspense," in *Beyond Aesthetics: Philosophical Essays* (New York: Cambridge University Press, 2001), 254–269. For an alternative resolution to the problem, which rests on the proposal that suspense lies in the frustration of the reader's desire to intervene in the situation, see Aaron Smuts, "The Desire-Frustration Theory of Suspense," *Journal of Aesthetics and Art Criticism* 66, no. 3 (Summer 2008): 281–290.

NOVEL TO SCREENPLAY

1. J. K. Rowling, "When Steve Met Jo," *Blue Toad* (April/May 2011), https://bluetoad.com/article/When+Steve+Met+Jo /705240/67460/article.html.2q.

2. See the excerpts from Kloves's interview with Geoff Boucher, available at Scott Myers, "Written Interview: Steve Kloves ('Harry Potter')," *Go Into the Story*, 20 November 2010, https://gointothestory.blcklist.com/written-interview-steve -kloves-harry-potter-1c8319d9e1f9.

3. Kloves, paraphrasing Rowling, during an interview included in the Blu-Ray boxed set: *Creating the World of Harry Potter, Part 7: Story*, ed. Suzanne Chambré-Sternlicht, Warner Bros. Entertainment, 2012. Rowling is sitting next to Kloves, and she agrees with him.

4. Michael Sragow, "Working Movie Magic—Steve Kloves's Scripts Make Potter Films Fly," *Baltimore Sun*, 4 June 2004, 1D; Glenn Whipp, "Cuarón Sharpens, Not Worships, Rowling's Work," *Chicago Tribune*, 4 June 2004, https://www.chicago tribune.com/news/ct-xpm-2004-06-04-0406040337 -story-html.

5. The movie also eliminates an unnecessary subplot involving Sir Cadogan replacing the Fat Lady as the guardian of the entrance to Gryffindor. However, Kloves's script does cover this subplot, and the deleted scenes on the Blu-Ray indicate that the subplot was filmed.

6. On locking the conflict, see Irwin R. Blacker, *The Elements of Screenwriting: A Guide for Film and Television Writers* (New York: Collier's Books, 1988), 7; and Darsie Bowden, *Writing for Film: The Basics of Screenwriting* (New York: Routledge, 2013), 30.

7. Rowling, *Prisoner of Azkaban*, 156.

8. Rowling, *Prisoner of Azkaban*, 226.

9. Rowling, *Prisoner of Azkaban*, 271.

10. This model synthesizes the recommendations offered in various books. See below for citations regarding specific traits. I have drawn particular inspiration from the ideas of Frank Daniel, whose theories are summarized in David Howard and Edward Mabley, *The Tools of Screenwriting: A Writer's Guide to the Craft and Elements of a Screenplay* (New York: St. Martin's Press, 1995).

11. In the movie Lupin steps in after the boggart has taken the form of a dementor. In the book he prevents Harry from taking part in the exercise entirely. Rowling, *Prisoner of Azkaban*, 139.

12. On turning points in general and midpoints in particular, see Kristin Thompson, *Storytelling the New Hollywood:*

Understanding Classical Narrative Technique (Cambridge, MA: Harvard University Press, 1999), 31; and Richard Krevolin, *How to Adapt Anything into a Screenplay* (Hoboken, NJ: John Wiley, 2003), 28. Note that Thompson favors a four-act model, with the midpoint acting as an additional breaking point.

13. On questions, answers, hopes, and fears as screenwriters' concepts, see Howard and Mabley, *Tools of Screenwriting*, 37–38; and Paul Joseph Gulino, *Screenwriting: The Sequence Approach* (New York: Continuum, 2004), 10–11. For a more theoretical approach to questions and answers, see the "erotetic" model of film narration in Carroll, "Toward a Theory of Film Suspense," 97.

14. On darkest moments, see Paul Lucey, *Story Sense: A Screenwriter's Guide for Film and Television* (New York: McGraw-Hill, 1994), 63; and Kate Wright, *Screenwriting Is Storytelling: Creating an A-List Screenplay that Sells!* (New York: Perigee, 2004), 7.

15. On third-act twists, see Linda Seger, *Making a Good Script Great*, 2nd ed. (New York: Samuel French, 1994), 19; and David Howard, *How to Build a Great Screenplay: A Master Class in Storytelling for Film* (New York: St. Martin's Griffin, 2004), 292.

16. Kloves, quoted in Jim Hemphill, "'I'm Not Qualified for Anything Else': Writer/Director Steve Kloves on *The Fabulous Baker Boys* and *Flesh and Bone*," Filmmaker.com, 17 September 2015, https://filmmakermagazine.com/95677-im-not-qualified -for-anything-else-writerdirector-steve-kloves-on-the-fabulous -baker-boys-and-flesh-and-bone/#.XyCByPhKjcM.

17. Steve Kloves, "Harry Potter and the Prisoner of Azkaban," Full Tan Draft, 24 February 2003, 18. I do not know if this was the last draft of the screenplay, but it is fairly close to the finished film. The copy may be found online at https://www .gazette-du-sorcier.com/IMG/pdf/Azkabanscript.pdf. For the relevant passage in the book, see Rowling, *Prisoner of Azkaban*, 73.

18. Kloves, "Prisoner of Azkaban," 67. The scene unfolds differently in the book. Ron and Hermione ask Harry if he wants to kill Sirius, and he does not answer. Rowling, *Prisoner of Azkaban*, 214–215.

19. Although Kloves deserves great credit for these changes, some critics have argued that he made certain other female characters—notably, Ginny—weaker than they were in the books. See Christopher E. Bell and Celina Smith, "Transmediated Weasleys: A Tale of Two Ginnys," in Bell, *Transmedia Harry Potter*, 105–117.

20. Rowling, *Prisoner of Azkaban*, 339.

21. Kloves, "Prisoner of Azkaban," 92.

22. Rowling, *Prisoner of Azkaban*, 396.

23. Kloves, "Prisoner of Azkaban," 109.

24. Kloves, "Prisoner of Azkaban," 117.

25. "And then it hit him—he understood." Rowling, *Prisoner of Azkaban*, 411.

26. "Harry's face changes. A riddle unravels." Kloves, "Prisoner of Azkaban," 119.

27. Field is the most prominent advocate for the view that all screenplays should follow the three-act model. He writes, "Do all good screenplays fit the paradigm? Yes." See Syd Field, *Screenplay: The Foundations of Screenwriting*, rev. ed. (New York: Delta, 2005), 28.

28. Marie-Laure Ryan, *Possible Worlds, Artificial Intelligence, and Narrative Theory* (Bloomington: Indiana University Press, 1991), 151.

29. Ryan, *Possible Worlds*, 156.

30. For a detailed list of doubles as they appear across the entire series, see Shira Wolosky, "Mirror Images," in *The Riddles of Harry Potter: Secret Passages and Interpretive Quests* (New York: Palgrave Macmillan, 2010), 99–126.

31. Ryan, *Possible Worlds*, 155.

32. Ryan, *Possible Worlds*, 156.

33. Ryan, *Possible Worlds*, 156.

34. Kloves, "Prisoner of Azkaban," 33, 39, 66, 92, 100, 108, 122, 125. Some of these lines are different in the finished film.
35. Aside from *Order of the Phoenix*, most of the remaining films follow the books more closely in terms of focalization. For instance, the book *Goblet of Fire* opens with a scene that appears to violate the limited-perspective approach (Voldemort's murder of the gardener), only to reveal that Harry experienced the scene in a dream. The rest of the book uses Harry as a fallible filter. The movie follows suit, starting with the gardener's murder and then sticking with Harry the rest of the way. The book *Half-Blood Prince* is more expansive, relating two key events that Harry cannot witness before switching back to Harry's point of view. The movie develops a similar shift, starting out unrestricted and then shifting toward restriction.
36. Cuarón, quoted in Whipp, "Cuarón Sharpens."
37. The wording in the Kloves screenplay differs from the wording in the finished film. See Kloves, "Prisoner of Azkaban," 43–44. Both scenes differ from the comparable scene in the book, where Snape interrupts the conversation before it turns to Harry's parents. See Rowling, *Prisoner of Azkaban*, 156.
38. The motif recurs in several other films—most notably, in *Deathly Hallows Part 2*, when yet another father figure, Snape, says it before he dies.
39. Rowling, *Prisoner of Azkaban*, 415. As in the previous example, the wording in the available screenplay differs from the wording in the finished film. See Kloves, "Prisoner of Azkaban," 122.
40. Kloves, "Prisoner of Azkaban," 121.
41. Andrew McGonigal, "Truth, Relativism, and Serial Fiction," *British Journal of Aesthetics* 53, no. 2 (April 2013): 165.
42. For two classic accounts of television narrative, see Michael Z. Newman, "From Beats to Arcs: Toward a Poetics of Television Narrative," *Velvet Light Trap* 58 (Fall 2006): 16–28; and Jason Mittell, *Narrative Complexity in Television* (New York: NYU Press, 2013).

43. Skeptical fans often wonder why Harry and Hermione do not use the Time Turner to solve more problems. The fifth volume, *Order of the Phoenix*, eliminates the issue by destroying all remaining Time Turners in a climactic battle. The play *Harry Potter and the Cursed Child*, written by Jack Thorne from a story by Rowling, Thorne, and John Tiffany, reframes the issue again, first by noting that previous Time Turners could rewind time for no longer than a few hours, and then by introducing a new and more powerful Time Turner that causes catastrophic setbacks.

44. Groves, *Literary Allusion in Harry Potter*, 8.

45. On Harry's transformed relationships with his father figures, see Kate Behr, " 'Same-as-Difference': Narrative Transformations and Intersecting Cultures in Harry Potter," *JNT: Journal of Narrative Theory* 35, no. 1 (Winter 2005): 118.

CAMERA, PERSPECTIVE, AND POINT OF VIEW

1. For the initial positive reviews, see Richard Corliss, "When Harry Met Sirius," *Time*, 7 June 2004; Peter Travers, "Harry Potter and the Prisoner of Azkaban," *Rolling Stone*, 24 June 2004; Leah Rosen, "Harry Potter and the Prisoner of Azkaban," *People*, 14 June 2004; and Owen Glieberman, "Wand Ambition," *Entertainment Weekly*, 11 June 2004. For more recent assessments, see Adam Chitwood, "Why 'Prisoner of Azkaban' Is the Best 'Harry Potter' Movie," Collider.com, 4 June 2019; and Nerdwriter (Evan Puschak), "Harry Potter and the Prisoner of Azkaban: Why It's the Best," Youtube .com, 13 January 2016, https://www.youtube.com/watch?v=3hZ_ZyzCO24.

2. Deborah Shaw, *The Three Amigos: The Transnational Filmmaking of Guillermo del Toro, Alejandro González Iñárritu, and Alfonso Cuarón* (Manchester: Manchester University Press, 2013), 173.

3. Vera Cuntz-Leng, "Look . . . at . . . Me: Gaze Politics and Male Objectification in the Harry Potter Movies," in *Transforming Harry: The Adaptation of Harry Potter in the Transmedia Age*,

ed. John Alberti and P. Andrew Miller (Detroit: Wayne State University Press, 2018), 86.

4. Sternberg, "Mimesis and Motivation," 453. Given the importance of the Proteus Principle to Sternberg's account, it is important to add that there is no necessary linkage between the camera's spatial perspective and the appeal to perspectival understanding. Camera placement may be motivated in many ways, and many techniques may be motivated according to perspectival logic.

5. In a previous book, I have discussed challenges and benefits of applying this model to camera movement in particular. See Keating, *Dynamic Frame*, 208–214.

6. Wilson, *Narration in Light*, 87.

7. Keating, *Dynamic Frame*, 46.

8. Rowling, *Prisoner of Azkaban*, 33.

9. Rowling, *Prisoner of Azkaban*, 165.

10. Rowling, *Prisoner of Azkaban*, 165.

11. Daniel Morgan, "Where Are We? Camera Movements and the Problem of Point of View," *New Review of Film and Television Studies* 14, no. 2 (2016): 238. Morgan has elaborated on this theory in a new book, the manuscript of which I read while I was finishing this volume. See Daniel Morgan, *The Lure of the Image: Epistemic Fantasies of the Moving Camera* (Berkeley: University of California Press, forthcoming).

12. Cinematographer Michael Seresin reports that the camera crew used wide-angle lenses for almost the entire film, including lenses as short as 14mm. See Patricia Thompson, "A Wizard Comes of Age," *American Cinematographer* 85, no. 6 (June 2004), https://theasc.com/magazine/june04/cover/index.html.

13. In the book Harry says the line to Ron. Rowling, *Prisoner of Azkaban*, 105.

14. In the book this conversation is between Harry and Dumbledore. Rowling, *Prisoner of Azkaban*, 425.

15. Michael K. Johnson, "Doubling, Transfiguration, and Haunting: The Art of Adapting Harry Potter for Film," in Anatol, *Reading Harry Potter Again*, 210.

16. On motifs, see David Bordwell, Kristin Thompson, and Jeff Smith, *Film Art: An Introduction*, 12th ed. (New York: McGraw-Hill, 2020), 63.

17. For technical details, see Thompson, "Wizard Comes of Age."

18. For technical details, see Benjamin B [Bergery], "Humanity's Last Hope," *American Cinematographer* 87, no. 12 (December 2006): 60–75. For analysis, see James Udden, "Child of the Long Take: Alfonso Cuarón's Film Aesthetics in the Shadow of Globalization," *Style* 43, no. 1 (Spring 2009): 26–44.

19. For technical details, see Benjamin B [Bergery], "Facing the Void," *American Cinematographer* 94, no. 11 (November 2013), https://theasc.com/ac_magazine/November2013/Gravity /page1.html. For analysis, see Bruce Isaacs, "Reality Effects: The Ideology of the Long Take in the Cinema of Alfonso Cuarón," in *Post-Cinema: Theorizing 21st-Century Film*, ed. Shane Denson and Julia Leyda (Falmer: REFRAME Books, 2016), https://reframe.sussex.ac.uk/post-cinema/4-3-isaacs/.

20. I argue that this tension has shaped Hollywood cinema since the studio days in Keating, *Dynamic Frame*, 39, 86, 189.

21. As other critics have noted, the sculpture of the eagle and the serpent may be read as Cuarón's allusion to the flag of Mexico. See Philip Nel, "Lost in Translation? Harry Potter, from Stage to Screen," in Heilman, *Critical Perspectives on Harry Potter*.

ACTORS AND AUTHORSHIP

1. McCabe, *Harry Potter Page to Screen*, 88.

2. McCabe, *Harry Potter Page to Screen*, 102.

3. According to one profile piece, "Ian Rankin recalled bump-ing into [Rowling] one day in an Edinburgh café: 'It was incredible to see her, writing longhand, doing this family tree for a character. I can't think of any other author I know who would go into that kind of detail for something that's not going to be there on the page.'" Ian Parker, "Mugglemarch," *New Yorker*, 24 September 2012, https://www.newyorker.com /magazine/2012/10/01/mugglemarch?currentpage=all.

4. McCabe, *Harry Potter Page to Screen*, 102.

5. McCabe, *Harry Potter Page to Screen*, 103.

6. Malcolm Turvey, *Play Time: Jacques Tati and Comedic Modernism* (New York: Columbia University Press, 2020), 20–23. Turvey raises a number of objections to Berys Gaut's multiple-authorship view. These objections create plenty of room for Turvey's single-author approach to operate, while leaving open the possibility that some films are multiply authored.

7. See, for instance, the discussion of "traffic jam" movies—that is, movies for which a film company hires and fires a series of filmmakers who are unable or unwilling to coordinate with one another—in Paisley Livingston, *Art and Intention: A Philosophical Study* (New York: Oxford University Press, 2005), 80.

8. Gaut, *Philosophy of Cinematic Art*, 101–102. For other defenses of multiple authorship, see Sarah Kozloff, *The Life of the Author* (Montreal: Caboose Books, 2014), 45–47; and C. Paul Sellors, "Collective Authorship in Film," *Journal of Aesthetics and Art Criticism* 65, no. 3 (Summer 2007): 263–271. It should be noted that while some of the sources I cite in this section disagree with each other on certain fine points, they agree that multiple authorship is a possibility worth considering.

9. Gaut, *Philosophy of Cinematic Art*, 117.

10. Gaut, *Philosophy of Cinematic Art*, 128.

11. Sondra Bacharach and Deborah Tollefsen, "*We* Did It: From Mere Contributors to Coauthors," *Journal of Aesthetics and Art Criticism* 68, no. 1 (Winter 2010): 23–32. Italics in the original title.

12. Andrew Sarris, *The American Cinema: Directors and Directions, 1929–1968* (Boston: Da Capo Press, 1996), 31.

13. Lubezki, quoted in Charles McGrath, "A Circuitous Route to Outer Space," *New York Times*, 3 January 2014, https://www.nytimes.com/2014/01/05/movies/awardsseason/alfonso-cuaron-discusses-his-films.html?_r=0.

14. Pamela Robertson Wojcik, "Typecasting," *Criticism* 45, no. 2 (Spring 2003): 244.

15. Christine Schoefer, "Harry Potter's Girl Trouble," *Salon*, 13 January 2000, https://www.salon.com/2000/01/13/potter/.

16. Dresang, "Hermione Granger and the Heritage of Gender," 223.

17. Rowling, *Prisoner of Azkaban*, 337–345.

18. Elizabeth E. Heilman and Trevor Donaldson, "From Sexist to (sort-of) Feminist: Representations of Gender in the Harry Potter Series," in Heilman, *Critical Perspectives on Harry Potter*, 146. For a more positive account of the series' representation of gender, see Glenna M. Andrade, "Hermione Granger as Girl Sleuth," in *Nancy Drew and Her Sister Sleuths: Essays on the Fiction of Girl Detectives*, ed. Michael G. Cornelius and Melanie E. Gregg (Jefferson, NC: McFarland & Co., 2008), 164–178. For an account that finds multiple ways to read the texts, see Ximena Gallardo-C. and C. Jason Smith, "Cinderfella: J. K. Rowling's Wily Web of Gender," in *Reading Harry Potter: Critical Essays*, ed. Giselle Liza Anatol (Westport, CT: Praeger, 2003), 191–205.

19. Andrew Klevan, *Film Performance: From Achievement to Appreciation* (London: Wallflower, 2005), 9.

20. Rowling, *Order of the Phoenix*, 518.

21. Some fans disliked one of Gambon's angry line readings in *Goblet of Fire* so much that they created GIFs repairing the mistake. See Katharine McCain, "*Epoximise!* The Renegotiation of Film and Literature through *Harry Potter* GIF Sets," in Alberti and Miller, *Transforming Harry*, 120–123.

22. James Naremore, "Notes on Acting in Cinema," in *An Invention without a Future: Essays on Cinema* (Berkeley: University of California Press, 2014), 49.

23. David K. Steege, "Harry Potter, Tom Brown, and the British School Story," in Whited, *Ivory Tower and Harry Potter*, 143.

24. Rowling, *Order of the Phoenix*, 821.

DESIGNING A WORLD

1. Perkins, "Where Is the World?," 22.
2. Perkins, "Where Is the World?," 25.
3. This episode is in the film but not in the corresponding book.
4. On dangling causes, see Thompson, *Storytelling in the New Hollywood*, 12.
5. I learned this fact on the Harry Potter studio tour.
6. See, for instance, Gillan Lasic, "There's a Painting of Voldemort in 'Prisoner of Azkaban,' and, Like You, We Want to Know Why," *Pop!*, 11 December 2017, https://pop.inquirer.net/44611/voldemort-painting-harry-potter-prisoner-of-azkaban.
7. Craig, quoted in McCabe, *Harry Potter Page to Screen*, 325.
8. McCabe, *Harry Potter Page to Screen*, 330, 337.
9. As Michael K. Johnson explains, the recurring time imagery echoes Rowling's recurring use of the word "time" (and assorted synonyms) throughout her book. Johnson, "Doubling, Transfiguration, and Haunting," 211.
10. Rowling, *Prisoner of Azkaban*, 101–102.
11. See also the book's introduction of the Shrieking Shack. Only after Harry and Hermione illuminate the space with their wands does Rowling provide a description of the "disordered, dusty room." Rowling, *Prisoner of Azkaban*, 337.
12. Temime, quoted in McCabe, *Harry Potter Page to Screen*, 104.
13. For details, see McCabe, *Harry Potter Page to Screen*, 100, 106.
14. Mary Ann Skweres, "The Real Magic of 'Harry Potter and the Prisoner of Azkaban,'" *Animation World Network*, 24 June 2004, https://www.awn.com/vfxworld/real-magic-harry-potter-and-prisoner-azkaban.
15. Mina, quoted in McCabe, *Harry Potter Page to Screen*, 517. She is referring to the Golden egg in *Goblet of Fire*, but the remark applies to many designs across the series.
16. Skweres, "Real Magic."
17. Jonathan Trout, "Alfonso Cuarón: *Harry Potter and the Prisoner of Azkaban*," BBC, http://www.bbc.co.uk/films/2004/06/01/alfonso_cuaron_azkaban_interview.shtml.

18. Seresin, quoted in Thompson, "Wizard Comes of Age."

19. Cuarón, quoted in Trout, "Alfonso Cuarón."

20. Russell Baillee, "Michael Seresin, the New Zealander Who Filmed Harry Potter," *New Zealand Herald*, 9 July 2004, https://www.nzherald.co.nz/lifestyle/news/article.cfm?c_id=6&objectid=3577493.

21. Seresin, quoted in Thompson, "Wizard Comes of Age."

22. For more technical details, see Thompson, "Wizard Comes of Age." The article features interviews with Cuarón, Seresin, and visual effects supervisors Roger Guyett and Tim Burke.

23. To this list may be added Oscar-winner John Seale, who photographed the first movie.

24. Chatman, *Coming to Terms*, 9. I discuss this and the following passages from Chatman in Patrick Keating, "Light and Time in the Narrative Fiction Film," *Journal of Cinema and Media Studies*, forthcoming.

25. Chatman, *Coming to Terms*, 9.

26. Chatman, *Coming to Terms*, 40.

27. See, for instance, Peter Verstraten, *Film Narratology*, trans. Stefan van der Lecq (Toronto: University of Toronto Press, 2009), 9.

28. Chatman, *Coming to Terms*, 31.

SOUND DESIGN AND MUSIC

1. Deborah Thomas, *Reading Hollywood: Spaces and Meanings in American Film* (New York: Wallflower, 2001), 97. For a classic account of these terms, see Bordwell, Thompson, and Smith, *Film Art*, 291.

2. Sternberg's basic contrast is between mimetic and aesthetic motivation, but he proposes various analogous pairings: world-like vs. rhetorical, referential vs. communicative, fictional vs. functional. See Sternberg, "Mimesis and Motivation," 364, 368.

3. Motivation is a kind of integration—that is, a "sense-making mechanism." Sternberg, "Mimesis and Motivation," 412.

4. Thomas, *Reading Hollywood*, 99.

5. Michel Chion, *Audio-Vision: Sound on Screen*, 2nd ed., trans. Claudia Gorbman (New York: Columbia University Press, 2019), 85.

6. Like the previously cited Meir Sternberg, Yacobi has discussed the contrast between perspectival motivation and existential motivation in depth. She situates them within a five-part account of the various mechanisms that readers use to make sense out of seeming incoherence. See Tamar Yacobi, "Narrative Structure and Fictional Mediation," *Poetics Today* 8, no. 2 (1987): 336.

7. See the detailed analysis in Tom Day, "Harry Potter: Magic in the Music—Part 1," Youtube.com, 29 May 2020, https://www.youtube.com/watch?v=gIWQP4hNYCA. This is one of several excellent video essays released in the last few years on the music in the *Harry Potter* series. See, for instance, a three-part video by Jaime Altozano, "Why the Harry Potter Soundtrack Sounds So Magical," Youtube.com, 11 December 2018, https://www.youtube.com/watch?v=RYihwKty83A.

8. Day's discussion of Lockhart's music draws on another excellent video essay: Good Blood (Javed Sterritt), "Harry Potter: Hidden Messages in the Music," Youtube.com, 15 November 2016, https://www.youtube.com/watch?v=JQR6rkT1guo.

9. Day takes this position, which is also voiced in Sideways, "Harry Potter and the Musical Secrets of the Marauder's Map," Youtube.com, 29 December 2019, https://www.youtube.com/watch?v=8FQcuENRhJw.

10. For this more critical position, see Inside the Score, "Harry Potter: How NOT to Compose for a Series (Part 1 of 3)," Youtube.com, 18 August 2018, https://www.youtube.com/watch?v=8b7-3lOgb24. The author continues the argument in two follow-up essays.

11. On the film's variety of musical styles, see Emilio Audissino, *John Williams's Film Music: Jaws, Star Wars, Raiders of the Lost Ark, and the Return of the Classical Hollywood Music Style* (Madison: University of Wisconsin Press, 2014), 227.

12. Audissino, *John Williams's Film Music*, 125. See also the analysis of a Williams score in Kathryn Kalinak, *Settling the Score: Music and the Classical Hollywood Film* (Madison: University of Wisconsin Press, 1992), 192–202.

13. Matthew Bribitzer-Stull, *Understanding the Leitmotif: From Wagner to Hollywood Film Music* (Cambridge: Cambridge University Press, 2015), 7.

14. Bribitzer-Stull, *Understanding the Leitmotif*, 14.

15. Bribitzer-Stull, *Understanding the Leitmotif*, 28.

16. Bribitzer-Stull, *Understanding the Leitmotif*, 271.

17. Bribitzer-Stull cites this example in his discussion of Williams's leitmotivic scores. He points out that the theme, which he names "Harry's Longing for Familial Love," becomes major in this scene. See Bribitzer-Stull, *Understanding the Leitmotif*, 285.

18. An illustration of the theme appears in Bribitzer-Stull, *Understanding the Leitmotif*, 291. The repeated note is an E, and its closest neighbors are F and D♯. Bribitzer-Stull explains that the theme reworks elements from two themes that had appeared in the previous films: the Mischief theme and a second theme associated with the Weasleys.

19. Sideways, "Musical Secrets of the Marauder's Map."

20. Sideways, "Musical Secrets of the Marauder's Map."

21. For more on Rowling's wordplay, see Cockrell, "Harry Potter and the Secret Password," 23. Also note that the film's credits list Trelawney's first name as "Sybil." In the book her first name is spelled slightly differently, as "Sybill." Rowling has explained that the name evokes both "Sibyl" (a female clairvoyant) and "Sybil" (an unfashionable English name). See J. K. Rowling, "Sybill Trelawney," Wizarding World.com, 10 August 2015, https://www.wizardingworld.com/writing-by-jk-rowling/sybill -trelawney.

22. Thomas, *Beyond Genre*, 20.

CONCLUSION

1. On paratexts and authorship, see Catherine Grant, "Auteur Machines? Auteurism and the DVD," in *Film and Television after DVD*, ed. James Bennett and Tom Brown (New York: Routledge, 2008), 101–115. See also the discussion of del Toro as auteur in Shaw, *Three Amigos*, 46, 56.

2. Radcliffe, quoted in the behind-the-scenes documentary *Creating the Vision*, produced by Michael Crawford, Warner Bros. Entertainment, 2004. The remaining quotations in this paragraph come from the same documentary.

3. *Conjuring a Scene*, produced by Michael Crawford, Warner Bros. Entertainment, 2004; and *Care of Magical Creatures*, produced by Michael Crawford, Warner Bros. Entertainment, 2004.

4. Perkins, "Where Is the World?," 26.

Index